The *Influential Leader*

*Using the
Technology of Our Minds
to Create Excellence in
Yourself and Your Teams*

*By
Rebel Brown*

All rights reserved. No part of this book may be reproduced or transmitted in any form or by any means, electronic or mechanical, including photocopying, recording or by any information storage and retrieval system without written permission from the author, except for the inclusion of a brief quotation in a review.

Published in the United States.

Copyright 2013

By Rebel E Brown
www.rebelbrown.com

All content and information in this ebook is based on various research into the human mind. That said, all thoughts are my own and as such, are opinions.

*This book is dedicated to those who taught me
the power of my very own mind.*

Adriana, Tad, Shalee and Stephan

You rocked my world. I am forever grateful.

Readers Say

"Modern times demand modern leadership approaches. And that's why *The Influential Leader* is so important. Rebel Brown shares eye-opening insights into the technology of our minds that leader must have to lead others. The Influential Leader is every leader's handbook for creating the influence and motivation we need to fuel breakout performance in their teams and in themselves."

John Baldoni
Chair, Leadership Development Practice, N2growth,
Author, *Lead with Purpose*

"Rebel Brown shares a unique passion in her book, *The Influential Leader – How to Use the Technology of our Minds to Influence and Win*, to fight against dehumanizing our minds at work. She lays out unique pathways and fosters choices that fuel increased productivity, innovation and collaboration regardless of where you stand at the moment. Readers who run with Rebel's notion of *technology of our minds*, will become transformational leaders that shift tired approaches into new-era opportunities. If you find yourself wondering what the human brain has to do with your own life or business success – read this book and you'll reboot your old passions into measurable tools for a finer future."

Ellen Weber PhD
Director, Mita International Brain Center

"Rebel Brown's new book is both insightful and instructive – a masterful work every leader should read. Modern neuroscience offers powerful insights into human motivation, thinking and behavior, and *The Influential Leader* applies these discoveries to deliver practical leadership practices that promise to deliver breakout results for ourselves, our teams and our organizations."

Mike Myatt
CEO N2growth, *Forbes* Leadership Columnist and Author, *Hacking Leadership*

"Neuroscience is about to have profound influence in many aspects of human endeavor. Recent, current and future discoveries in neuroscience will change how we live. They will certainly change leadership. *The Influential Leader* is the first book I have read to clearly show the way for this new transformative leadership path. If you want to be a successful modern leader, reading this book is the essential first step."

David Houle
America's Leading Futurist

"What would it mean to your own leadership talents if you could tap the underlying brain science at work with your peers and staff? And what if you could share these essential insights with the leaders throughout your organization, so they could multiply your newfound ability to make success happen? Now you can, with Rebel Brown's pathbreaking new ebook, *The Influential Leader*. Read it – *consume* it, as I did! Transform your understanding. Transform your business. "

Ted Coine
Co-CEO, SwitchandShift.com

Readers Say

"Rebel Brown's books offer outstanding advice from a dynamic individual who has proven herself in the business world, and her forthcoming book, *The Influential Leader,* is no exception! With neuroscience-based insight into the workings of the human mind, Rebel demonstrates how to better motivate your team, inspire change and performance, and communicate effectively with varying personalities. This book will guide you through shifting the way you think and act in order to become an inspired, passionate leader!"

Angela Maiers
CEO, YOU MATTER, Speaker, Writer,
Passionate Educator

"Long-held beliefs about leadership theory and practices just got expanded by *The Influential Leader.* Rebel Brown presents a compelling, fact-fueled, research-supported leadership book, sharing how we can integrate more of our humanity into how we lead by understanding how our minds work. If you are interested in improving how you lead, you definitely need to read this book."

Shawn Murphy
Co-CEO, SwitchandShift.com

"Fascinating! The more you know about what makes people tick, the more effective your leadership *can* and *will* become. Read this book!"

Frank Sonnenberg
Former National Dir. of Marketing, Ernst & Young
Management Consulting
Author, *Managing with a Conscience*

"If you're a leader or a visionary manager, *The Influential Leader* is an important read. A thought-provoking look at how our minds are programmed, and how we can change that programming to produce new and better results."

Randy Gage
Author of the New York Times bestseller,
Risky Is the New Safe

"When I started reading Rebel's book I hoped it was going to be great because this is a subject close to my heart. I am pleased to say it isn't great. It's Brilliant! Rebel takes complicated details and explains them with metaphor and examples in such a way that this book can be read and used by academics, students and novices alike. My only complaint is she wrote it 20 years after I was looking for a book like this when I started in this business! Highly recommended."

Dave Moore PhD
The Moore Consortium,
Creator of Human Potential Technology

"Reading *The Influential Leader* is a must for leaders who seek to survive and thrive this "Transformation Decade"; a decade where the imperative to optimize the power of our minds, the power of our ability to ideate, communicate and collaborate faster and better has never been more important. Kudos, Rebel Brown for providing leaders and organizations with a new neuro-business launching point, a practical and powerful guidebook for motivating, innovating and actualizing results that are driven by the power of our minds to learn, communicate and lead forward.

Irene Becker
CEO, Just Coach It, Developer of the 3Q Edge

"Rebel has done it again. OMG, I couldn't stop reading *The Influential Leader*. It is simple but yet profound. This book invites you to upgrade your mindware and delete century old files that no longer work. Most importantly, she gives you tips, tools, and techniques on how to Shift Into Action. Read it, Do it, and Pass it on."

Simon T. Bailey
Leadership Catalyst, Brilliance Institute and
Author, *Release Your Brilliance*

"*The Influential Leader* is a must read for any leader who wants to create high performance teams. By applying the powers of neuroscience to our own leadership styles, we can and will fuel new levels of employee performance, productivity and most importantly, job satisfaction."

Jane Perdue
Leadership Futurist

Rebel Brown mixes neuroscience and common sense to enable you to shift your thinking and transform your leadership. *The Influential Leader* will reprogram the technology guiding your unconscious mind freeing you to become the leader and the person you always wished you could be!

Mike Henry
Sr. Chief Instigator, Lead Change Group

"*What if we could expand our minds to see new opportunities*" ... and with that opening sentence Rebel Brown captures the essence of creating success. Although she titles the book "The Influential Leader", this book is for every human with a dream of having a different life. You can read just the chapter headings in this book and immediately begin your new journey or sink into a chair and ponder the deeper meaning."

Kate Nasser
The People Skills Coach™

'Success starts with your story - and your story starts with your thinking. Understanding how your mind works is the way to understand how to make things work for you - and lead your teams in more powerful ways. Read this book, and understand where leadership really begins!"

Chris Westfall
Author of *The NEW Elevator Pitch* and *Bullet Proof Branding*

The Influential Leader shares key lessons from the latest scientific frontier—the human mind. The insights and lessons in this book give leaders the tools they need to achieve optimum performance, in themselves and within their organizations.

Susan Steinbrecher
Author of *Heart-Centered Leadership*

Are you ready to leverage creativity and innovation? In the *The Influential Leader*, Rebel Brown uncovers how our minds work to process information and make decisions. She demonstrates how we can re-wire our mindware to unlock new levels of collaboration and productivity. Pick this book up and begin shifting your thinking today.

Stan Phelps
Best-Selling Author, Keynote Speaker and Consultant

Rebel Brown is one of the best writers I've read on the subject of neuroscience and leadership. *The Influential Leader* shares key insights and provides practical methods to help leaders and their teams achieve peak performance. Get a copy for everyone one your team!

Jesse Lyn Stoner
Co-author *Full Steam Ahead! Unleash the Power of Vision* and *Leading at a Higher Level*

Table of Contents

Foreword 12

Prologue. 14

Introduction 16

Section One   It's All in Our Minds 21
Chapter 1: How Our Minds Really Work 22
Chapter 2: Leading the Survival Mind in Modern Times. 32

Section Two   Leading Breakout Performance 39
Chapter 3: I Know We're Right. 41
Chapter 4: Who Did What to Cause This? 44
Chapter 5: The Status Quo Bias 47
Chapter 6: The Sky is Falling 51
Chapter 7: We'll Knock it Outta the Park 54
Chapter 8: But We Never Saw This Coming. 57
Chapter 9: We All Agree .61
Chapter 10: But It's a Strategic Investment. 65
Chapter 11: It's Not My Fault 68
Chapter 12: There's Nothing We Can Do 71
Chapter 13: Everyone Agrees With this Plan 74
Chapter 14: We Know Best. 78
Chapter 15: That's My Job 81
Chapter 16: But That's the Way We've Always Done It 85
Chapter 17: Shifting Out of I 90
Section Two Summary 95

Section Three   What Makes People Tick? 99
Chapter 18: Insights from our Mindware 100
Chapter 19: What's Your Motivation Direction? 103
Chapter 20: Everyone Has a Preference 106
Chapter 21: The Why Behind What We Do 109
Chapter 22: What Does it Take to Convince You? 112
Chapter 23: Sorting Our World 117
Chapter 24: How We Frame Our Decisions 120
Chapter 25: What's Your Chunk? 123
Section Three Summary 127

Table of Contents

The Bottom Line 130
About The Author 131
Resources 132

Foreword

We live in a new millennium, a new century, a new age and a still new decade. This unprecedented alignment means that we are in a time of incredible, transformative change. The speed of change has accelerated to the point where we live in an environment of continuous and accelerating change. What was acceptable and expected ten, five, even three years ago is no longer the reality.

When the world, business and the marketplace are in such a dynamic state, old ways of doing business, reliable management dictums and theories no longer work. Suddenly they all feel tired. What we need are new ways of looking at the world, new ways to motivate people, new ways to create highly successful teams, and new ways to quickly embrace and implement change.

This book gives us just that.

As a futurist I have spoken around the world about the fact that legacy thinking of the 20th century has propelled us into this new century. I have written and spoken about how humanity has left the Information Age and entered the Shift Age. I coined the name Transformation Decade for this 2010-2020 decade. The definition of transformation is 'a change in nature, shape, character or form' which means that in this decade most of humanities institutions and ways of thinking will change. This means that if you are a CEO or a leader of an organization, and you are not actively changing its' nature, shape, character or form, it will fall behind and may not exist in 2020.

How to create this change?

One way is by utilizing new information about how our mind works and how we can integrate this knowledge into the living of a life or the leading of a team or company.

Foreword

Neuroscience has had incredible breakthroughs just since the beginning of this new century. We have learned more in this time about the mind than in all the time before. We now understand better than ever how we think, how we process information, how we are wired. This means that now, for the first time we can put incredible new scientific insights into our minds to work in making what we do and how we do it better.

The Influential Leader is the best book I have read that does exactly this. Rebel Brown has integrated these new insights from Neuroscience into her proven methods of motivation, change and leadership. This combination is not just powerful; it is a new paradigm for change leadership today. I simply cannot imagine any leader, manager or even self- aware person consuming this book and not taking away something that will, in fact, positively and profoundly impact their situation.

Are you ready to change? Are you ready to find new ways to more fully utilize your mind and then integrate this into new, enlightened ways to lead? Are you ready to enrich those you lead and infuse them with greater understanding and passion?

If yes, then turn the page.

David Houle,
October 2013

Prologue

Why will we follow the herd, even if it's right off the cliff?

Why is clear communication so elusive among humans?

Why are some folks so easy to motivate, and others just plain difficult?

Why does the prospect of change transform intelligent humans into irrational beings?

Why do we fail to see the opportunities, and challenges, that are right in front of our eyes?

We've all seen these patterns of behavior, heard the limited thinking in our businesses. We've also felt the frustration they cause. Regardless of the organization, business model, market or products, we all experience these same patterns as leaders.

Why?

I kept asking myself that question every time I'd see the patterns in my consulting work. Why do we do this and think that? Why do intelligent professionals seem to don blinders when it comes to business and professional performance?

I had to know. So I began my study of neuroscience. What I learned changed my perspectives on we humans in business, and in life, forever. It will change yours too.

I've worked with leading edge technology firms for over two decades. Yet in my study of the human mind through neuroscience, I found the most magnificent technology of all – the technology of our minds. I learned that the power to change beliefs, step into limitless thinking, create a new reality, and more, is all in our minds.

Imagine influencing your teams to harness that power into breakout business and professional results. You can. Starting right now. That's why I wrote this book.

Why Does Neuroscience Matter to You?

Whether you're an entrepreneur starting your own business, a CEO of a large corporation, or the leader of a team, you are leading *humans in business.* Thanks to neuroscience - the technology of our minds - you can learn how to influence and lead people into the next generation of productivity, performance *and* satisfaction.

That's why neuroscience matters to you.

Neuroscience discoveries are turning traditional beliefs about how we think and behave upside down and insight out. The more you understand your amazing human mind, the more you *will* confidently throw traditional leadership beliefs into the wind. There is a better way to lead.

This book shares twists and turns within our human minds that explain the thought and behavior patterns leaders face every single day. When you apply this powerful information to your business, you step into a whole new world of leading and motivating your team to success.

The technology of our minds is the path to the next generation of human performance, in every aspect of business *and* life. That's why I'm shifting my career focus to share this amazing technology with you. You can influence your teams to transform your business. You can create excellence in everything you do.

You have the ability to step into your limitless potential, and the potential of your teams. It's right there, in your mind!

Introduction

Imagine:

> *Turning your teams into high-performance machines.*
>
> *Understanding what makes your teams tick, then using that information to fuel breakout results.*
>
> *Engaging every individual to step beyond the way they've always done it to power profitable innovation.*

You can do this and much more, thanks to the power of our minds.

Neuroscience, the study of the technology behind the human mind, is sharing amazing new knowledge that empowers modern leaders to fuel the next generation of business performance. From breakout business results to professional and personal success, the power to step into leadership excellence that drives bottom line results is right there waiting for all of us – in our minds.

When we lead in a manner that matches the ways our individual minds function, the results are nothing short of extraordinary. By learning how the human mind works, then applying that information to individuals and teams, leaders can and will influence new levels of productivity, performance, engagement, innovation and employee satisfaction.

We're learning more about the technology of our minds every day. In many cases, research is proving that traditional theories about how we humans operate are not necessarily accurate. For example, we traditionally assumed that we humans are rational creatures dominated by our conscious, logical minds. We now know that *isn't* the case. Our unconscious minds drive 90- 95% of our[1] decisions and behaviors. Often, we don't even know it.

Modern leaders have the opportunity to adopt leadership approaches that leverage the human mind to influence breakout results. The only question is, *"What does it take to step into this opportunity?"*

This book shares lessons and knowledge from a number of neuroscience fields, applied to leadership in our modern world.

- First we'll learn about the technology of our minds and how we really think and respond.

- Then we'll discuss specific mindware programs that often limit our business behaviors and decisions. What's mindware? Just as computers have software, our brains have mindware, powerful programs that drive our thinking and behaviors. In many ways these programs get in the way of our success. We'll learn how to fuel motivation, innovation and growth by shifting our organizations and employees beyond these limiting programs.

- Next we'll learn about the fundamental mindware programs that drive human behaviors. We'll examine how to leverage these programs to support and inspire your individual team members to reach for new levels of productivity and success.

How to Use this Book

We are leading humans in business. Every human mind is unique, so no two leadership situations are alike. Yet whether we're working with individual employees and teams or peers and management, we can call on neuroscience to help us influence for a positive result.

This book is designed as a reference book for influential leaders in any situation. It shares information and discoveries about the technology of our minds, applied to a variety of leadership scenarios.

Each chapter is organized to discuss a) the mindware program that drives a specific behavior or thought process and b) the shift leaders can make to influence beyond these limiting mindware programs and into next generation results.

Different chapters in this book will be applicable to your specific leadership needs at any point in time.

You have a choice in how you read and use the information to step into influential leadership.

- You can choose to read the entire book, then go back and apply the lessons to your leadership roles as they unfold.
- You can choose to only read the chapters that are relevant to your leadership scenarios today, then read other chapters as new scenarios unfold in your daily leadership life.
- At the end of Section Two and Three you'll find summary tables that capture the key content of each chapter in an easy-to-use reference guide for the section.

The following table is a guide to help you select the specific information that is applicable to your leadership role today, and tomorrow. Since many chapters are applicable to a number of leadership needs, you'll see chapters repeated in the table.

LEADERSHIP FOCUS	CHAPTER (S)
Understanding the Human Mind	1: How Our Mind Really Works 2: Leading the Modern Survival Mind
Stepping Into Responsibility	9: Leaving the Herd Behind 11: Be the Cause, Not the Effect 12: Blame Begone 20: The Why Behind the What 23: How We Frame our Decisions

Introduction

LEADERSHIP FOCUS	CHAPTER (S)
Fueling Innovation and Creativity	4: Model Success 5: Ditch the Status Quo 8: Shuffle that Deck 9: Leaving the Herd Behind 16: Forget that Rearview Mirror 17: Shifting out of the I
Improving Communication	9: Leaving the Herd Behind 18: What's Your Motivation Direction? 21: What Does it Take to Convince You? 24: What's Your Chunk?
Supporting Collaboration and Teamwork	9: Leaving the Herd Behind 15: Team Beats Turf 22: Sorting Our World 23: How We Frame our Decisions 24: What's Your Chunk?
Driving Next Generation Productivity	4: Model Success 7: There's Upside in the Downside 8: Shuffle that Deck 19: Everyone Has a Preference
Instilling a Positive Focus	4: Model Success 6: From Half Empty to Overflowing 12: Blame Begone 20: The Why Behind the What
Customer-Driven Thinking	13: Challenge that Consensus 14: Ask Your Buyers 15: Team Beats Turf
Objective Business Decisions and Goals	7: There's Upside in the Downside 10: A Dollar is a Dollar 13: Challenge that Consensus 23: How We Frame Our Decisions

www.RebelBrown.com

LEADERSHIP FOCUS	**CHAPTER (S)**
Motivation and Inspiration	4: Model Success
	6: From Half Empty to Overflowing
	18: What's Your Direction?
	19: Everyone Has a Preference
	21: What Does it take to Convince You?
	24: What's Your Chunk?
Matching People to Their Best Jobs	17: Insights into Our Mindware
	18: What's Your Direction?
Hiring the Best Person for the Job	19: Everyone has a Preference
	20: The Why Behind the What
	21: What Does it take to Convince You?
	22: Sorting Our World
	23: How We Frame Our Decisions
	24: What's Your Chunk?

Whether you read the entire book, or choose to select specific information, the more you understand about the inner workings of our human minds the more powerful your leadership can and will become.

The power to influence our teams to breakout human performance is ours. It's right here - in our minds.

Section One

It's All in Our Minds

What Every Leader Needs to Know About the Technology of the Human Mind

Chapter 1

How Our Minds Really Work

The more we learn about our minds the more we find a complex and highly sophisticated machine. We also discover that the keys to leading this machine to deliver peak performance are often very different from traditional beliefs about leadership.

Modern research gives us deep and powerful insights into the technology of our minds. These insights dramatically enhance how we communicate, collaborate, think, analyze and solve problems. These same discoveries share new perspectives on motivation, inspiration and the performance of individuals and organizations.

Why Leaders Should Care About the Technology of Our Minds

Modern science has proven that our unconscious minds drive the vast majority of our behaviors and decisions. That's right. *We are guided by our unconscious minds in more ways than we ever knew.*

Imagine understanding why your teams' unconscious minds process and respond as they do. Now imagine knowing how to communicate directly to influence every employee across your organization to reach and then exceed their human potential.

How can you step into that powerful level of influence? By matching your leadership style to the way each individual's mind is programmed to think and respond.

When you apply the technology of our minds to your leadership, you will:

- Inspire your teams to new levels of innovative and creative thinking.
- Create the ideal work environment so that each team member excels.
- Assign roles and responsibilities that exactly match each team member's skills, thinking and motivations.
- Motivate the entire team to engage in clear and compelling communication and collaboration. Then motivate the entire organization to do the same.

These are a few of the benefits leaders will gain when they understand and apply the power of the human mind to create highly influential leadership.

The Technology of Our Minds

Let's start with a simple overview of how our minds work.

Quantum biologists have learned that our minds are powerful quantum machines. Out of massive amounts of data and limitless potential combinations, we select a tiny piece of incoming information as our reality. We also use automated mindware programs to determine many of our responses, behaviors and decisions.

Why does that matter to leaders? Because every person you lead has their own unique programs that serve to create their own unique reality. When you understand how to recognize and influence these programs, you bring your teams into alignment in the way they think, focus, direct their time and energy and create results.

Here's a basic overview of how our minds work.

Think of your mind as a massive supercomputer.

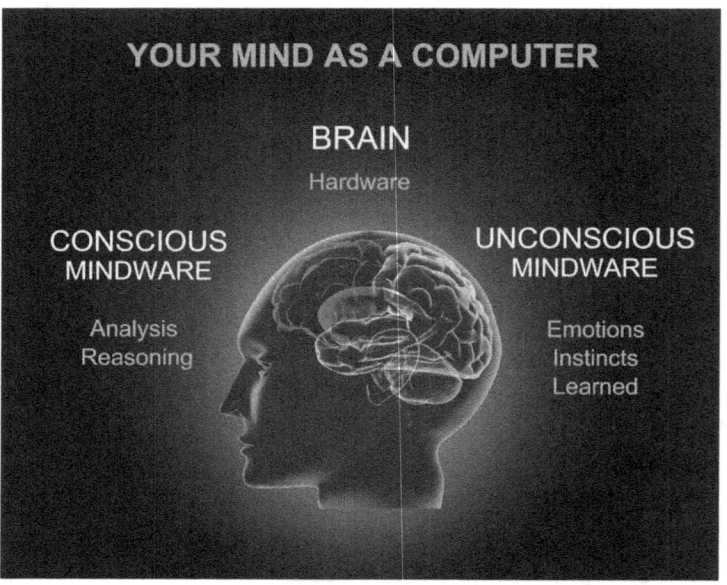

- Your brain is the hardware system, like a laptop or that iPad you love so much.

- Your conscious and unconscious mindware is the software that drives your hardware, aka your brain.

- Our conscious mindware is created through our learning and experience. We are aware of these programs since we use them proactively every day to do everything from math to reading to solving a business issue.

- Some of our unconscious mindware programs are with us at birth, for example the preference programs we all have that form the unconscious infrastructure of our behaviors and responses. We tune these infrastructure programs based on our early childhood experiences and lessons. Every combination of preference programs is unique to our own experiences as we finalize the tuning of these programs. (We'll learn more about preference programs in Section Three.)

- Other unconscious mindware programs are created and updated throughout our lives, based on our experiences, decisions, values, attitudes and beliefs. That's why none of us have the same mindware programs. Our programming is as unique as our individual lives.

Together, our conscious and unconscious mindware drives our thoughts, beliefs, decisions and behaviors.

We are not the conscious, logical beings we've been trained to believe.

> ***In fact, our unconscious is the master of our conscious mind and our reality.***

How's that for a shift in how we humans actually work?

Your Quantum Mind in Action

The many worlds theory of quantum mechanics[2] states that there are limitless optional outcomes (past and future) in any situation. Yes, quantum theory tells us that we can indeed change the outcomes from our past to shift our reality today.

Imagine an infinite number of paths stretching out in front of you, each leading to a different result. Quantum mechanics postulates that we select one of those paths to act upon as our reality.

How do we select the specific reality we choose to experience?

Our unconscious mind is in charge of processing all of the data we take in from our five senses. It decides which data to select as our reality, based on our specific expectations, point of focus, state and mindware programs.

If our unconscious mind – not our conscious mind – is responsible for our data selection, management and storage, how do we know that what our conscious mind receives as reality is really what's real?

Think about that one for a minute…

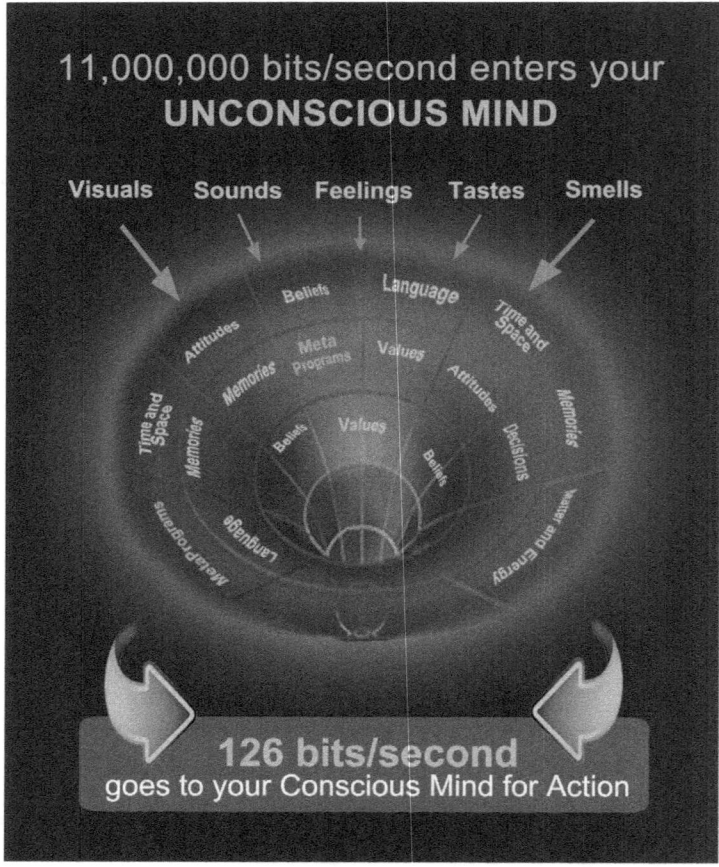

The figure above shows how information flows through your unconscious mind. You unconscious filters this massive information to present only what it sees as important to your conscious mind for processing and action.

Here's how the flow works:

Data Inputs. We take in over 11 million bits/second of sensory information[3] from our eyes, ears, feelings, noses, mouths and overall thoughts. Now stop and think about that for a minute. That's a LOT of information to process every single second of our lives.

We have to manage that vast stream of sensory information before we respond to any of it. If we didn't manage and prioritize it, we'd be stuck processing information forever. We'd never actually do anything.

Data Selection. From that 11 million bits/second, our unconscious mind selects 126 bits/second to give to our conscious mind for processing and action. Read that again. It's a big number to comprehend, isn't it? Here's an analogy.

Imagine a stack of toothpicks over a mile high. Then select 2 inches of those toothpicks. That's the equivalent of our unconscious mind selecting our reality from all of the sensory data we collect.

That 126 bits/second represents .0000122 of the total information available to us at any moment in time.

Talk about selective attention!

What about all that other information we take in?

How many other realities are there in that 10.9+ MB of data we ignore?

What if we could expand our minds to see new opportunities, notice expanded markets, take advantage of emerging trends that others cannot see?

We Select Our Unique Reality

Our unconscious uses mindware programs including our Preference Programs (See Section Three for more information), Values, Beliefs, Decisions, Memories and Attitudes to select our reality.

These mindware programs join our current focus and expectations to determine the specific information we select from our sensory data stream as our current reality.

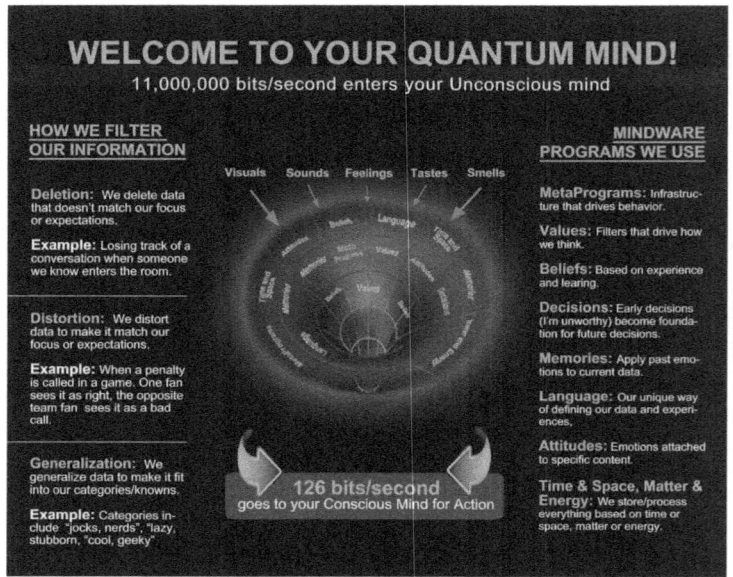

Guided by our mindware, our unconscious mind uses the processes of deletion, distortion and generalization to select the data we send to our conscious mind for action.

Deletion. We delete information that doesn't match our expectations or focus.

We've all experienced the power of deletion. At a party or networking event you're chatting with someone who, well, isn't exactly holding your attention. As your mind wanders you notice someone you really want to meet enter the room. Then your conversation partner asks, "*What do you think?*" You realize you have no clue what he or she just said. OOPS.

That's the power of deletion. Your unconscious mind deleted the piece of incoming sensory data from your conversation partner in favor of your new focus, in this case the person who walked into the room.

This same deletion action occurs in team meetings, one-on-one meetings, customer meetings, in researching an assumption and pretty much anywhere and everywhere we are inputting information.

Imagine how much information is deleted when you're sharing insights, requirements, details, roles, responsibilities and objectives with your teams?

Now think of the results when you're able to communicate in a manner that assures each and every team member retains the key insights and information they need to create success for the team, the organization and themselves?

That's the power of influential leadership.

Distortion. We distort information to make it fit into the expectations and focus that match our unconscious mindware.

We are familiar with the power of distortion in our lives. Take that big football game between two conference rivals you watched with friends who were avid fans for each side. Remember that foul call that changed the momentum of the game? One buddy thought it was the best call possible (his team benefited). Your other friend saw a totally mistaken call by the referee. (Yep, he's for the other team.)

Or maybe you saw a movie with friends and afterward it was as if they saw a different scene or maybe even a different movie.

That's the power of distortion in action. We distort the data that creates our reality to match our expectations and focus.

As a leader, what if you could communicate and share information in a way that breaks through the distortions that limit your teams' vision? What if you could shift beyond the expectations and focus created by the past and into an open field of creativity and insights?

That's the power of influential leadership.

Generalization. Our unconscious mind creates categories and buckets that make information processing more efficient.

Some of these categories are created by our social upbringing and parents, other categories are created by our experiences in our lives.

Say you see someone in ragged clothing walking down the street pushing a shopping cart filled with odds and ends. You probably think "homeless." You see a giant of a man with huge muscles and the build of a football player enter a coffee shop. You probably think "professional athlete," associated with your favorite local team.

Such generalizations are all around our unconscious mind. We use these categories and buckets to quickly generalize our information into something we already know. The problem is that we're often mistaken. The homeless person is an actor researching his role. And the athlete is a nurse at the local hospital.

Imagine how many times this program causes us to profile a customer, competitor, prospect or co-worker, missing the key details that really matter? Now think about the power of leading your teams to step beyond the assumptions and into the power of truth.

That's the power of influential leadership.

The possibilities are endless, right there waiting to be engaged, right there in our minds.

No Two are Alike

Quantum mechanics[4] has proven that scientists see what they expect to see when they look into a high-powered microscope. If they expect to see a particle of matter, they see that particle. If they expect to see a wave of energy, they see the wave.

The same thing is true of each of us. We all choose our own unique reality from our vast ocean of sensory information.

We make that selection using our own unique mindware programs and filters.

That means we each live in a reality of our very own selection, a reality that we choose and interact with based on our own individual mindware. No two realities are alike since no two humans have the same mindware programs. Now that explains a lot, doesn't it?

Our quantum minds explain why multiple people respond to the same stimulus with multiple and very unique perspectives. Talk to anyone about a recent meeting or conference and you'll get as many perspectives as you have people. The same goes from every interaction or experience in our professional and personal lives.

The Bottom Line

When we understand that each individual has his or her own unique perspective of what's real, we can evolve the way we see our teams, hear their comments and profile their skills. The more we understand about our human minds, the better we can influence others to step into their ultimate performance.

As leaders, understanding how our quantum minds work is especially important today. That's because another powerful program is being triggered more than ever in our modern world. This program dramatically impacts our team's productivity and performance. Once we understand how to lead beyond this program, the results are nothing short of spectacular.

This program is called survival mind.

Chapter 2

Leading the Survival Mind in Modern Times

The push to do more faster than ever, financial concerns, shifting markets and businesses in flux create an unpredictable world. Then there's the media's focus on fear-based news, not to mention the shoot-'em-up movies, games and more, all of which serve to trigger our threat responses.

What's a threat response? We humans respond to situations we perceive as threatening with instinctual programs stored in our unconscious, what I call our survival mindware, which are instincts created by our caveman ancestors.

As modern humans, our minds are still programmed with a survival principle learned in the earliest days of humans: *A missed threat is more important than a missed opportunity.* That principle was critical to caveman survival. Who cares if there's some food out there if a cougar is lurking in the bushes? Pay attention to the cougar!

In our modern world, survival mind gets in the way of performance, productivity and communications. You see, our survival instinct is triggered everywhere we turn. And that's a big and very limiting problem.

Survival mind was designed by nature to protect us from intermittent threats. In caveman times we had breaks between the threats for our minds to move out of survival mode, recover and return to normal processing.

In today's world we do not get those breaks. In fact, we're continually bombarded with stimuli that trigger our survival mind. We have no chance for recovery or that so important "reset." That means that many of us are operating in a continuous state of survival thinking and responses.

That's bad news for business.

When survival mind is active we focus on keeping ourselves in the safety zone, aka the status quo or the way we've always done it. We don't even know we're in survival mode. When a threat is perceived by our unconscious mind, our brain sends a chemical error message[5] into our system that creates physiological discomfort. That's why we push away from progress or change in the name of survival, because that change or progress is perceived as a threat.

That instinctual response sidetracks our rational and progressive business decisions. When a change is presented – even a positive change – our threat response is triggered. We move into unconscious responses and hunker down in the safety and comfort of the way we've always done it, instead of embracing new ideas and approaches,

The issue is that human creation and innovation comes from our conscious minds. When our unconscious survival mind is triggered, our conscious mind cannot engage.

Creativity and innovation ceases as survival mind is continuously triggered by our modern world.

Only when we lead our teams to step fully into their powerful conscious minds can we fuel ultimate innovation and productivity.

That's why influential leaders will lead our teams away from survival mind and into conscious creativity, fueling next generation performance.

That's also why it's important to take a hard look at our traditional beliefs about leadership approaches and techniques.

Traditional Leadership Triggers the Survival Mind

Many traditional leadership approaches are founded in a reward-and-punishment paradigm. That fear-based paradigm often serves to escalate human survival responses, especially in today's already over-sensitized humans.

Some traditional leadership approaches are easily perceived as threats by our unconscious minds. For example:

The Stick. First let's look at the "or else" threat, or stick, that's part and parcel of traditional pressure to perform, deliver, succeed.

Motivating with fear adds more threat triggers to the already heightened survival response in our modern world. When we apply the stick, many of our employees and teams will react by holding more tightly to unconscious and ineffective survival responses that include:

Hanging onto the status quo, which is viewed to be the safety zone.
Freezing in fear, resulting in the inability to think out of the box, meet that schedule or deliver expected performance.

Avoiding the change entirely as the mind's error messages and associated physiological discomfort push us away from anything but safety.

Some people do need an "away" stimulus, aka something to move away from, to become motivated. In these cases, a small stick may be appropriate – but only if a person has a mindware program that will positively respond to that small stick. We'll learn how to determine the appropriateness of an "away" stimulus in Section Three.

We only should use a stick when it's appropriate and not as a blanket approach to motivation. For many of us humans, the stick simply doesn't work to increase performance. In fact, it does just the opposite.

Competition among teams. We've all worked for bosses who believed that pitting one person or team against another was the path to success. I've always thought this was just plain silly. The competition is outside the business. That's why they're called our competition!

Team competitions create divisions that set the stage for infighting instead of innovation. Turf and/or fight-or-flight response takes over as productivity declines. The majority of energy is spent defending within our own company instead of competing in the external world. That's not the recipe for success. Nor does it open our minds to become more creative, innovative or motivated.

As leaders we have the opportunity to focus on creating integrated, high-energy teams committed to serving our customers. We can do that by asking questions and designing processes so that our teams come together to form a whole that is greater than the individual parts. We'll learn more about that in Section Two.

The Push for Innovation. *"We need a new idea and we need it now!"* We've all heard it, that pressure to come up with the next breakout idea, right this minute. As if we can all snap our fingers and turn on our creativity program.

When we're stressed we have difficulty thinking creatively and outside the box. Why? Because our survival response keeps us stuck in our unconscious mind. We need our logical, conscious mind to be online and active to imagine and deliver creative thinking. We cannot be creative and stressed at the same time.

Our conscious mind can only tap into its innovative capabilities when our unconscious mind tells it that there is no threat in our environment.

As influential leaders we must quiet the unconscious survival mind to empower innovative results. That means removing stresses, pressures and negative potentialities that threaten our teams. If we want true innovation, we need to be innovative leaders who create positive environments for our teams. We need to deliver what they need to be productive and creative. We'll learn more about this in Section Two as well.

The Carrot. Incentives and rewards are based on the assumption that given the proper direction and motivation, a person will do as directed.

Yet our unconscious mind will behave adversely to this approach when survival mind is dominant. Remember, a threat is more important than an opportunity. No matter how big the incentive, in an uncertain world filled with threats and danger that carrot pales in comparison to the prospective new threat. The threat wins and we ignore the carrot.

As influential leaders, it's our job to determine the best motivation for the individual and then consciously use that motivation to inspire innovation and performance.

It's time we forget the blanket approach to leadership and manage individuals as the unique people we all are.

The Bottom Line

If we're all in a state dominated by our unconscious survival mind, how can we be effective leaders?

How can we work with the unconscious minds of our teams to fuel their optimal productivity, performance and that feeling of safety humans need to do their best?

> ***By understanding and leading based on instinctual human behavior and the power of our unconscious minds, we can all be successful leaders.***

We can adapt our leadership styles to match the needs of our employees to inspire, motivate and fuel positive results. That's one of the most powerful aspects of applying the technology of our minds to leadership.

How do we make that shift? It's all in our minds ... right there, waiting for us to step into a new way of thinking and communicating.

By simply acknowledging the power of our unconscious mind, we take the first step toward recognizing the shift in today's workforce. Then we can employ into leadership styles that break through the programmed responses to communicate clearly, motivate and successfully fuel next-generation productivity and performance.

The rest of this book shares a number of shifts that leverage the power of neuroscience applied to leadership, in business and in life.

Apply these shifts with yourself and your organization. You'll see, hear and feel the difference in your teams and your results.

I guarantee it!

Section Two

Leading Breakout Performance

Using the Technology of Our Minds to Influence Individuals and Teams

How do we shift our leadership approaches to leverage the power of our unconscious minds? How do we lead beyond the limiting programs that create drag on our business results?

Let's start by exploring a few mindware programs that are present in nearly every human being on this planet.

This section shares a selection of unconscious programs that drive our actions and thoughts. Each program is an embedded part of the technology of our mind – specifically our unconscious human thinking and responses.

When we step into conscious leadership with these programs in mind, dramatic and powerful results *will* follow.

In each chapter you'll find an overview of the program and recommended leadership shifts. Apply these shifts as a influential leader, business professional, sales person and marketing force and in your everyday life.

You'll see, hear and feel the powerful results.

Chapter 3

I Know We're Right

Mindware Program
We assume we're right and seek out the evidence to prove it.

Leadership Shift
Consciously find the evidence to prove yourself wrong.

What if your research on a new strategy, product or assumption gave you new insights that fueled even more powerful and positive results?

That's exactly what happens when you shift your perspective to search for evidence to prove yourself *wrong*.

We've been taught in business school and our professional lives that research is critical to success. We spend so much time doing research, listening to industry luminaries and asking questions of our markets. But what answers are we seeking?

Our usual approach is to prove that our assumptions are correct. Think about the last time you hopped on the web to search for information about an assumption you want to check out. Did you type in a search looking for information to prove the inaccuracy of your assumption? Or did you seek information that supported your stance?

We all are programmed to prove ourselves right. That's because of an inherent mindware program[6] that suggests we *are* right – no matter what we think or believe. We'll believe we're right *unless* we consciously step up to question that unconscious programming.

Influential Leadership: The Benefits of Being Wrong

By choosing to seek information that proves ourselves wrong, we shift our perspectives. We change our mindware program to see more clearly and objectively with that simple shift. Plus we get a number of additional benefits:

- <u>We loosen our programming</u> around whatever topic we're researching. This empowers us to expand our perspectives and take in new insights and information. We get a more balanced perspective on the assumption or strategy, resulting in a better end result.

- <u>We find the evidence of potential problems</u> in our belief or theory *before* we move forward, saving time and money and that big headache. Isn't it better to shift a strategy or assumption before we invest in it? That surely beats having to jump through hoops to salvage whatever we can on the other side of a less than optimum strategy, plan or product.

- <u>We often find even more powerful options</u> for success as we seek evidence to disprove our initial belief. When we look at the evidence without needing to prove ourselves right, we find tidbits and nuances that help us create an even better result.

- <u>We find we're right.</u> If we don't find any evidence to dissuade our assumption that we're right, chances are high that we're on to something great!

Shift Into Action

As leaders, we can instill a powerful new model of thinking for ourselves, other leaders, and our teams.

Here's how.

The next time you're researching into an assumption about your products, your markets, your business model or whatever else you might be doing, shift your team's focus.

- Set a goal for your team to <u>seek out information that is contrary</u> to your assumption or strategy.

- Actively and visibly <u>seek that same contradictory information yourself</u> – through research and market interactions.

- Readily <u>accept and act upon contrary evidence</u>, adapting your baseline assumptions to embrace an ever-changing environment.

- <u>Reward those team members who find new insights</u>, contrary information or additional ideas that improve on your baseline assumption.

The more openly we explore and research our theories and postulates, the more likely we are to find the best possible options for success. With these four simple actions, we set a powerful model for teams and other leaders to do just that.

Chapter 4

Who Did What to Cause This?

Mindware Program
We spend the majority of our time focused on fixing problems, so much so that we miss new opportunities.

Leadership Shift
Focus on finding what is working, then model that success. Also spend more time seeking new opportunities.

What if you could guide your team and organization to model the successes all around us? What if you focused entirely on what's working instead of nitpicking and focusing on all of the problems? Imagine the power in that perspective as you create success after success after success?

As influential leaders, we can shift our perspectives to create just such a success-focused environment. We simply have to become aware of our unconscious mind's tendency to constantly look for threats. And then, we shift!

Cavemen needed to look for the threats that were all around them. In our modern world, constantly seeking the problem or threat is inappropriate. In fact, our obsession with searching for what's wrong and for picking at everything is downright counter-productive.

We all know a seagull leader – the one who swoops in, points out every single nitpicky problem and then moves on to his or her next victim. That's not a recipe for motivation or success, is it?

Influential Leadership: Focusing on Success

Great influential leaders focus on modeling the successful behaviors of others. Yes, they notice the problems and issues in their teams and organization, but they don't dwell on them. They address them and then re-focus on success.

They look for what is working and then model that success in other aspects of their lives and business. For example:

- Instead of habitually looking at the bad, consciously shift into focusing on what's working.
- Look within your own team, within other teams and outside of your organization to other businesses and industries.
- When you find great successes, explore the "why" behind them. Then apply what you learn to your own teams.

This shift may seem simple, but it's powerful. Studies have proven that we do indeed experience what we focus upon. So when we focus on problems, we experience more problems. When we focus on successful models, we imprint those very same models on our own organizations and selves. Success follows.

Shift Into Action

So you shift your focus away from problems to find models of success. Now what do you do? As you find these models that you want to apply to your business:

- Understand their values and beliefs about the successful behavior, process or thinking that you want to model. Question them about their priorities and what was important to them, what they believed to be true about their success. Then, model those values and beliefs in your own world.

- Ask them about their strategy for success. What did they do specifically and in what sequence? What were they holding as their definition of success? Learn the answers and then apply them to your own situations and thinking.

- Get to know their own personal beliefs about their success. How do they hold themselves, what are their thoughts and emotions? Modeling someone's excellence includes the more human sides of the equation as well.

Aside from looking for success outside of your organization, look inside for the best work your teams deliver. Teach them to look for what's right and to work within the team. Focus on those successes and look for other successful models across the organization that you can adopt.

Once you understand these insights, begin to shift your own leadership thinking and behaviors to match the successful models. Then lead your teams to match those same behaviors and thought processes too.

One of the powerful aspects of our human minds is our ability to model the behaviors and thinking of others to upgrade our mindware. When we focus on modeling success, positive results can and will follow.

Chapter 5

The Status Quo Bias

Mindware Program
Status Quo Bias – hanging onto the way we've always done it.

Leadership Shift
Make the status quo a threat, then seek new options.

What if your teams were eager to embrace all kinds of changes, including new ways of doing, thinking and believing? What if they shifted their thinking to proactively seek a new and better way in every aspect of their work?

Imagine the power of an organization thriving on change.

We've all experienced the opposite reactions, seen our teams dig in their heels and fight even minor changes. That's not stubbornness – it's a human mindware program in action.

Our unconscious minds hold onto the status quo because it's a safe port in the storm known as life. Survival mind drives us to hang onto what is known and safe. To step into our full potential, we must shift our thinking out of our unconscious status quo bias[7].

Influential Leadership: Beyond the Way We've Always Done It

The easiest and fastest way to shift any human away from the way we've always done it and into a place where we can think differently is to make the status quo unsafe.

- <u>Recognize that the status quo bias exists</u> and that we're being drawn to hang onto it. Once we recognize the status quo bias in action, we can begin the shift.
- <u>Take a moment to consciously ask questions</u> and notice all the threats, negatives, limitations and issues associated with that very status quo. When our unconscious minds see it as a potentially unsafe place, we begin to look for new options.
- <u>The same goes with teams.</u> Make the status quo less appealing by pointing out the challenges, the risks, the downside potentials of remaining in that very status quo. Then visibly reward those who step into new thinking. The combination will motivate teams toward new and conscious solutions.

By the way, I'm not talking about scaring your teams. That only increases the threats in their environment and fuels survival thinking. Be indirect and thoughtful in the way you shift the status quo. Adding more fear to the equation is not the best method of unhooking the status quo.

Shift into Action

We've all been trained to ask the typical questions in our businesses and lives. Who, what, when, where, and how are the traditional areas to explore. This isn't necessarily the best approach to opening our minds to move beyond our status quo bias and into innovation and creative thinking.

Why? Traditional business questions are designed to narrow our focus to the context of a specific thing in the present or past. Statements do the same thing to our minds – focusing and narrowing our perspective. Both statements and traditional questions tend to limit how and where our minds will search to discover the answers.

On the other hand, more open and general questions like "What if?" tend to free our minds to focus on possibilities yet to be discovered. Since I'm a big believer in ditching the status quo and opening to new and expanded choices and possibilities, "What if?" is fast becoming my favorite question of all time!

There are so many places to use this question in our professional and personal lives. Here are some of my favorite examples:

- <u>Problem Solving</u> Our traditional approach goes something along the lines of "Who did what? When and where did they do it? How did it happen?" In my experience I quickly learned that this line of questioning a) pointed the focus to the past and b) quickly turned into a blame game. That's not exactly productive, now is it?

    When we spin the focus to the solution and a positive future, the results become much more powerful. Simply ask such questions as:

    "What if we tried a new approach? What if we solved this issue while focusing on a sustainable future solution? How might that solution appear?"

- <u>Perceptual Conflicts</u> Your employee sees things one way and you see them another. Your associate reads that email one way and you meant it totally differently. We've all been there. It's part of being human.

One of the fastest ways to get ahead of the potential conflict in such situations is to simply ask, *"What if I put myself in their shoes? What if I look thru their eyes and perspectives?"* By doing just that, we can shift our perspectives to include those of others and then bring all of that insight to bear on uniting in a common perception around pretty much any topic. From that place, we have the power to create amazing results that include all the perspectives.

- <u>Brainstorming</u> I wish I had a dollar for every brainstorming session that focused on the Who, What, When, Where and How of the past as a starting point for the future. It's the way we've all been taught to think.

  What if we changed it? Instead of starting with the way we've always done it, what if we began by asking the "What if?" question, focusing on innovation and new ideas in our future?

Sure, we have to add some practical insights based on the what's of our business. Yet beginning with a blank whiteboard is one of the most powerful ways to stimulate creative thinking. Asking the *"What if?"* question to fill that blank whiteboard with fresh perspectives and new ideas will fuel creativity and innovation.

Isn't that what brainstorming is all about?

Chapter 6

The Sky is Falling

Mindware Program
Our modern world is programming us to focus on the negative.

Leadership Shift
Model the ability to focus on and find the upside.

What if your teams were focused on the upside in every aspect of their work, from creating new products to identifying innovative approaches to beating the competition? What if "*We Can't*" was eliminated from your organizational vocabulary?

That's quite a shift from today's world. Have you noticed all the Eyore attitudes in our world today? Everywhere I turn I hear cries of doom and gloom. Use of the "can't" word has reached an all-time high.

The focus on hunkering down into defensive mode creates the perfect setup for failure. Worse yet, we often end up hanging on by a thread and wondering why things aren't getting better.

That's the power of our human programming to expect the worst.

Getting stuck in the stress and trauma of yesterday's economic shift won't help you lead your teams in the new economy. What's done is done. Our world shifted. And it's still shifting. And it will continue to shift.

Influential Leadership: Focus on the Upside

We all have the opportunity to identify new approaches and capture new opportunities for business growth. Or we can hunker down and live in contraction mode. It is our choice.

In every economic and market shift, new opportunities for successful growth appear. Those who focus on a market without limitations see and capture those opportunities. Those who stay stuck in survival mind flat line or crash and burn.

Leaders can motivate their teams into this powerful shift by modeling and rewarding the attitudes they want to see in their teams. We can consciously and effectively shed the Eyore eyes that limit our ability to see new opportunity. As leaders, it's our job to do just that.

Shift Into Action

How do we literally shift the way our teams see their world? It takes a combination of patience, creativity and time. Here are a few examples from clients.

- One leader started a Change box. Any team member who went "negative" contributed $1 to the box and then consciously re-stated the negative comment or approach with a positive, solution-focused statement. Before long, the team as a whole shifted into solution-oriented thinking. From there, they identified a major new market opportunity and the business was off and running into new growth.

- Another leader asked team members to bring a new success story from their market, or a related market, to every weekly team meeting. After sharing these success stories, they brainstormed about modeling what they'd learned to drive expansion or a better way within their own business. The team created a pin board to post great ideas found via their research. It didn't take long for them to find multiple paths to new opportunities while upgrading their thinking and approaches.

- One client created a "What if" board for new ideas. She asked all employees to post their ideas for new approaches and then worked with the executive team to select one idea from each department to implement every month. Within two months efficiency within the business had increased significantly, and employee morale had doubled.

As leaders we all know that a positive attitude has as much to do with productivity and performance as does our skill sets. That's why it's imperative that we take extra time, focus and energy to guide our teams away from the negative programming that's all around and into a focus on the opportunity, the potential and the upside for our business.

Chapter 7

We'll Knock it Outta the Park

Mindware Program
We tend to be overconfident of our abilities and results.

Leadership Shift
Add more downside to the scenario.
Test strategies under much wider scenarios.

What if you knew that your pipeline forecasts, product delivery schedules and every other projection around your business was dead- on accurate? They can be!

Just as we're programmed to be Eyores in some areas, we also have a program that makes us overconfident in others areas. We are such complex beings!

We've all seen that sales pipeline stuffed with hope. That's actually human nature. We are programmed to be overconfident[8] in our projections.

We can thank our caveman ancestors for that one. After all, you have to be confident to take on a saber-toothed tiger with a spear, just as you have to be confident to start a new business.

This mindware program has its upsides, especially if you're speeding into new and dangerous territories!

Influential Leadership: Balanced Expectations

It's much easier to manage a business when we have confidence in our timelines and goals. From accurate revenue pipelines, to product development schedules to cash requirements, the more accurate our projections, the better our results.

That's why it's important as leaders to balance our programmed overconfidence to prevent our natural tendency to overstate our potential results.

When it comes to running a business, it's always better to know the truth rather than make decisions based on hope.

Shift Into Action

Here are some ways to balance the negatives of this mindware to determine realistic goals and projections:

- Rather than look at best-case forecasts and all of the upside for our business, get critical. Pick apart those numbers and don't settle for anything less than reality.
- Ask questions and dig deeper into the facts. Be more flexible and build more options into your strategies and assumptions. Instead of one main business plan with small upsides and downsides, run three plans: Best case, most likely case and worst case. That way you'll already be prepared and thinking about multiple options and strategies.

- Ask people from a broader base of perspectives to review your scenarios. Instead of going back to the same "experts" again and again, seek new opinions from fresh eyes – inside and outside of your business and industry.
- By the way, don't offer three options. Studies show that people tend to pick the safe choice in the "middle" option. Instead, offer two or four options for discussion.[9]

It also helps to add 20% more downside to each assumption or scenario (and choose more pessimistic options while you're at it). This is especially important if those assumptions are critical to the bottom line of the business.

With our programmed optimism, the risk of getting the downside wrong is higher than miscalculating the upside.

So downsize your projections. It's a great thing to beat those numbers. After all, over-performing is a great problem to have!

Chapter 8

But We Never Saw This Coming

Mindware Program
We seek patterns in data and numbers, then we anchor to them.

Leadership Shift
Shuffle the deck! Change the way you see things!

Have you ever looked at a report or forecast and suddenly noticed a trend that was anything but positive? Then you wondered how in the heck you didn't notice it sooner?

Think about the benefits of being able to notice even the slightest shift in your business – before it becomes an issue. That's the power of shuffling the deck.

Our human minds actively seek out patterns. Patterns make it easier for us to process and respond to information. The more patterns we automate, the more efficient our mind becomes so that we can devote more attention to watching for threats.

The problem is that over time we only see the patterns of what we expect to see in our reports and data – not the real information that is in front of us.

- When we view/input information in the same format over and over again, we create a pattern that represents what our unconscious minds *expect* to see.
- When we continue to look at data or information in the same formats, we see what we expect from the past.
- We miss trends and shifts that portend significant changes in our markets and business.

Influential Leadership: Creating Fresh Perspectives

Shuffling the deck means changing the way we present our business data to our minds. It's a simple shift with big results. Why?

When you change the way you present your data, your unconscious mind sees a new format that doesn't match what it expects. So it calls for help from your conscious mind. That's when you see what's really on the page, slide, spreadsheet or pipeline report.

In the graphics below you see a standard spreadsheet and a scattergram. These graphics represent two very different ways to visualize information that gives our mind two very diverse perspectives.

By changing the format of our reports, forecasts, product timelines and other data, we open our minds to see important shifts and trends as they are happening and before those shifts create an issue or become a missed opportunity.

But We Never Saw This Coming

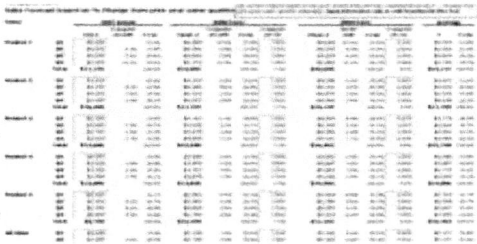

Traditional Data

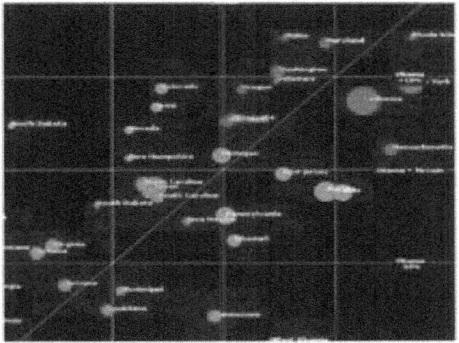

Shuffled Data

Shift Into Action

You already practice shuffling the deck today. Think about the different formats you try when you're presenting to your boss, prospect or board of directors. We seek the best visual format to best show what we want our audience to perceive. Sometimes growth or success is more compelling on a bar chart, sometimes on a line graph or sometimes on a pie chart.

Specifically, these shuffles will give you a fresh perspective on your business.

- Shuffle all of your decision-making information for a month. Then pay attention to the insights and trends you see.

- Shuffle the reports your managers receive. By changing the way they take in information, you'll change the way their brains see and analyze that data. New insights are sure to follow.
- Shuffle those revenue forecasts and the way you rate your prospects likelihood of buying. Change the categories associated with the likelihood of revenue, change how you profile your prospects and customers with regard to specific product purchases too. When you shift the parameters you create a new perspective on your business.
- Try focusing on bluebird market opportunities and never before seen applications of your product as the fuel for your revenue stream. Do an exercise in forecasting beyond your current normal customer forecast. Make the priority a focus on new and different opportunities and watch the perspectives change in your teams.
- Train your teams to shuffle, too, from the way they create their deliverables to the way they brainstorm new ideas. Their ability to see subtle changes and respond to those shifts will increase as well their ability to create new and valuable insights about the business.

Once you start shuffling, keep on shuffling. Your unconscious mind is constantly seeking and applying patterns. By making shuffling a continuous process, you'll keep your conscious mind engaged. You'll see the subtle changes that you can leverage to create big results.

Chapter 9

We All Agree

Mindware Program
Our unconscious mind rewards us for sticking with the herd.

Leadership Shift
Reward folks visibly who don't follow the crowd.

Have you ever wondered why your team steps into groupthink, tending to follow the lead of the most persuasive team member? What if you could eliminate that "follow the leader" thinking to inspire individuality and breakout thinking in every situation? Think about the new ideas and insights that would flow from this simple shift.

We tend to follow the herd, or group, because our minds dig conformity. On the flipside, our minds *dislike* behaviors or beliefs that differ from others.

Put those two ends of the motivational spectrum together and you have a powerful herd mentality[10]. This mentality impacts every decision we make – as a business professional and a human.

Our caveman brain (aka reptilian brain) holds our instinctual, deeply programmed responses, the things that are intrinsic to humanity. Our reptilian brain is designed to promote our safety and survival. That's probably why it creates triggers that motivate us to conform. After all, to a caveman or woman, conformity with the tribe was the baseline for survival.

Consequently, our unconscious minds automatically reward us with a pleasure response (thanks to a chemical naturally injected into our system) whenever we agree with the crowd. Our mind also sends an emergency alert response when we disagree with the crowd and begin to start out on our own course.

Welcome to the herd instinct.

Today, the herd instinct often limits innovation and ultimately performance. We've all experienced the power of a strong opinion to sway our teams, customer focus groups and more.

The Herd in Business

The implications on business behavior are monumental, both internally and externally. When we consciously understand and leverage the conforming brain, we can shift from following the conformity instinct to breakout thinking that creates significant and sustainable advantage.

The need for conformity explains the status quo we so often see within corporate cultures. Whatever leaders, bosses or the squeaky wheels believe becomes the corporate point of conformity, and everyone else follows along. Those brave souls who stand up against the conforming behavior are often viewed as rebels, troublemakers or simply uninformed.

Yet some of those who do step out and create a strong new opinion *can* capture followers because of the conforming brain – whether that new opinion is accurate or not. That's why strong personalities, or people who are viewed (rightly so or not) as gurus and visionaries, often capture the passion of their follower and sway our perspectives. In the extreme, such conformity can segregate our business focus, creating multiple groups with conflicting beliefs and behaviors, thus limiting our ability to successfully execute our specified strategy. *And we don't even know it.*

Have you ever noticed how a corporate culture tends to have a very few leading opinion creators and a large number of opinion supporters?

That's the conforming brain in action.

Influential Leadership: Beyond the Herd

What if you could lead your teams to step into the power of their individual creative minds, then join together to bring those ideas into fruition?

We can lead our teams away from the herd and into individual thinking.

Here's how:

- Model your behavior to show your teams that it's a good thing to step away from the herd and demonstrate individuality in thinking and actions. As a leader, come up with wild ideas, pushing the envelope farther than ever. The herd will be motivated to follow your model.

- Visibly reward team members who step away from the herd and into independent thinking. Even if the ideas aren't usable, reward the step into individual thinking and perspectives.

Shift Into Action

Let's say your business needs to make a change in the way it perceives its value in the market. Anyone who has ever led that type of shift knows how quickly herds form to protect the status quo, especially if there's a vocal leader protesting that change.

What can you do to quiet that herd and move people toward the change?

- Instead of focusing on the problem causing the change, <u>focus on the new opportunity</u> for the team thanks to the change. Show the team members the upside for success – visibly. By focusing on the solution and upside you shift the team away from the threat of the change (and the problem) and into the opportunity.

- <u>Set up a leader</u> who can be vocal in support of the change. Before you even communicate the change, get a team leader on board with the new idea. Show this person or people why the change is good for all, then give them the lead in promoting that change within the team.

- <u>Visibly reward</u> those who come on board with the change. Be sure the other team members are aware of the rewards and that they too can be part of the upside.

- <u>Ask the team</u> about the change. When folks are questioned and feel as if they are part of a change, they tend to shift into the change more easily. Ask them individually what they believe would be the best shifts they can make as part of the overall change, then support them in doing just that. As individuals move to embrace the change, so will the overall team.

The herd instinct can be a powerful tool in marketing, sales and when we want to create a cohesive team. The key is to balance the herd instinct and its potential survival mind instincts with the collaborative innovation and new approaches we need to be successful.

Chapter 10

But It's a Strategic Investment

Mindware Program
We associate different value with different investments.

Leadership Shift
Eliminate strategic versus tactical P&L categories, be sure to view all dollars spent as equal.

What if you knew that each and every financial decision in your business and your life was based on reality, not on the assumptions your mind makes based on its unconscious preferences? What, you didn't know you weren't doing that already today?

Richard Thaler coined the term "mental accounting," defined as *"the inclination to categorize and treat money differently depending on where it comes from, where it is kept and how it is spent.*[11]*"* For example, assume you have $50,000. How do you feel about spending that money for a new car? How do you feel about spending it to fix the roof and foundation on your home? Different feeling, huh?

The same is true in our businesses. We'll cap the spending on a mature division, even as we spend freely on a new idea or startup that we assume is going to be the next big thing. We even create new categories of spending to wrap investments in a more appealing manner. We think of "strategic investments" or "business development expenses" in a different way than we speak of "taxes" and "overhead."

The reality is that every dollar spent has the same value initially when it comes to that P&L.

Influential Leadership: No Specials Here

It's important to shift beyond the emotional responses to spending and stick with a simple rule: *Every Dollar is Worth a Dollar.*

Avoid categorizing dollar spends as strategic vs. overhead.

Review every expenditure in the same category on that P&L, and be especially cautious around anything dubbed as "startup," "strategic," or even "development." It's all the same when it leaves the bank.

Shift Into Action

"Mental accounting" can be found across all types and sizes of business. Even the most conservative leaders can find themselves stuck in mental accounting.

Examples of how to overcome this programming include:

- <u>Treat any and all expenses as equal dollars.</u> For example, if you're booking against a restructuring charge for your business, be just as concerned about that expense as you would be about a direct charge through your P&L. Restructuring is not a free or low cost lunch.

- <u>If you impose spending limits</u>, make them across the board. Just because a project is new and fun doesn't mean it gets to spend more dollars than a project that's more mundane and uninteresting.
- <u>Stick with the spending categories</u> you have in place and don't get creative. For example, there's a new trend to categorize dollars spent as "strategic" as if they were a different value than dollars spent on "overhead." Avoid this trap in thinking.

It's human nature to rationalize certain expenditures as somehow different from others. And yes, the Return on Investment can and does vary. That said, a dollar is a dollar when it comes to your bottom line.

Chapter 11

It's Not My Fault

Mindware Program
Seek something or someone to blame.

Leadership Shift
Be the Cause. Then teach your teams to do the same.

We all believe that we're taking responsibility for our lives. That's a good thing because taking responsibility is critical to attaining our goals.

Key to reaching our goals is our appreciation of cause and effect. In each and every life situation there is a cause, and there is an effect.

Personal and professional power comes from accepting the role as the cause for all experiences in our life. If we choose to be an effect, we become a victim to the world around us – the ex-spouse who cheated, the unfair boss, the economy, the government and other external influences become the cause in our lives. When we live as an effect we become more and more powerless.

Obviously that's not a good choice. Yet we make it, don't we? I surely did.

Until recently I would have gone to my grave believing that I was taking responsibility for my life. Then I learned I was fooling myself. When I understood the reality of cause or effect and then listened to my internal dialogue, I found myself sitting in the effect side of the equation in more areas that I would have ever guessed.

We are programmed to be *in effect* by everything from society to the media to our government to our entertainment. Look around and you'll see a wealth of comments, articles, news stories and more teaching us that we are single individuals at the mercy of this big world around us. In today's world we see people, groups, organizations and even entire societies living on the side of effect.

As leaders, it is imperative that we live and act on the cause side of our equation, modeling that powerful behavior.

We humans also set ourselves up to like living in effect. It's a natural (and not so inspired) part of our human programming. We focus on the problem and what's bad, wrong, ineffective or broken over and over again, giving the problems more power. As we think and focus, so we become.

Shift Into Action

To find my own place as the cause in my life, I started keeping a little notebook full of the statements I heard in my mind. about me, my life and all of its events. Every time I caught myself in the effect side of life I wrote down the thought. Then, I stopped and pivoted the thought to take the cause position, to be my own responsible party.

One of the principles I believe in is that we all have the resources we need to do whatever we want to do. I also believe that we are the cause of our lives. We can control our minds, and therefore we can control our results ... aka the effects.

I shifted to take responsibility for every effect (result) in my life. I am the cause, no matter what happens. There are no excuses. The buck stops here.

This single shift in perspective created powerful impacts in my life. More and more personal power is flowing because I claimed my position as the cause of all of my life's experiences, good and not so much.

Stepping up to be the cause in your life *will* give you more personal power. Try it for a week or two and you will be amazed at the difference in your own results.

Then, empower your teams with the knowledge to stand as the cause of each of their own effects. The results will be spectacular – for the individual, for the team and for your business.

Chapter 12

There's Nothing We Can Do

Mindware Program
When we feel like we're failing, we tend to blame external forces.

Leadership Shift
Find the feedback in the failure and focus on the coming success.

What if your teams were focused on results and moving forward, even when in the midst of failure (aka feedback)? Imagine the power applied to your business when the energy we put into placing blame is instead focused on evolving for future success?

One of our deeply engrained human thought processes drives us to focus on looking for the problem, for what's wrong and for someone to blame for it. By the way, this is also how our unconscious mind justifies sticking with the status quo.

Blame is one of the biggest challenges in a world that's uncertain and changing, especially when we feel powerless to control our external environment. By focusing on the mistakes and blaming someone, our brains give us the feeling of being in control. But that kind of control does not produce innovation or optimal performance.

While we're focusing on the problem and who to blame for it, we often can't see the solutions and new opportunities that are right in front of our faces. Aside from de-motivating those around us, we miss the positives in front of our eyes.

Influential Leadership: Relish the Feedback

As leaders we choose how we respond to situations. By focusing on the feedback instead of the failure, we model a powerful behavior.

That's why it's important to instill a new belief in our teams and across our organizations...

> *Failure is merely feedback that moves you closer to your ultimate success.*

When we change the way we look at "failure," we can and will motivate and inspire teams to change. Instead of focusing on the fear of failure and only stepping forward into "sure things" we can motivate our teams to create an advantage out of what could have been a de-motivating and threatening failure.

Shift Into Action

Here are a few techniques to shift into a gain versus a blame focus:

Focus on what's working well for your business. We all tend to pick at the problems, focus on what's wrong. We've been trained to do just that since the beginning of our careers.

Unfortunately that behavior programs our teams to focus on the negative as well. How can you be motivated to think creatively when you're focusing on the bad things? You can't. So shift your focus to what's going well and doing more of that. Your teams will follow suit.

As we shift into a focus on what's working and successful, we begin to model that thinking across all areas. That modeling opens our minds to see new options, think positively and generally become more creative.

Focus on what others do well, too. Performance is as performance does. So look at your competitors and model what they do well. Don't copy. Do use their positives to model your own innovation and ideas.

Be sure to look at companies outside of your industry as well. If you're a B2B business, you'll be amazed at the breakout ideas you can find in B2C marketing. If you're B2C, look at those B2Bs for innovation. Seek out the processes, behaviors and approaches that are driving success for others. Then, model them in your environment and get your teams excited about looking for great models outside of your industry. When they are exposed to new ideas and approaches, their creative minds are fueled and innovation follows.

When there is an issue or problem, flip it to the positive lesson learned. Adopt this simple principle for all of your teams.

There is no failure, only feedback.

Inside of every problem, mistake or just plain screw-up are the seeds of a solution. Focus on the lessons learned and that solution, not on beating the problem into submission. It's already done and gone: Focus on the upside. Teach your teams to do the same.

Chapter 13

Everyone Agrees With this Plan

Mindware Program
We assume consensus, even when we don't have it.

Leadership Shift
Test broadly, challenge assumptions.

Have you ever been knee deep in a project only to realize that there was dissension in the ranks? Or maybe you discovered that your bosses weren't as eager to support your approach as you thought, especially when the going got tough?

Welcome to the habit of assumed consensus. As humans, we are programmed to perceive that we have consensus[12] around an approach, idea, project, process and more.

Assumed consensus can result from groupthink caused by herd behavior, especially if the person proposing a belief or tact of action is a strong force in the team.

Assumed consensus can also result from selective recall in which we only remember what we choose to remember that proves our case.

Then there's the habit of only asking for an opinion from those who we know will agree with us. Yep, we stack the deck.

Assuming consensus is one of the biggest enemies of our businesses. I've seen it time and again in turnaround clients and beyond. It causes businesses to stay on the wrong course, move to a strategy that isn't well-founded and just plain get stuck in status quo thinking.

Influential Leadership: Challenge that Consensus

We all want to gain consensus and that's a good thing. We also want that consensus to be real. So how do we know the difference?

As leaders it's important to be very cautious with our leadership influence. Using it to drive a result we want is dangerous to the team and the business. Similarly, we need to be aware of those team members with clout and balance their ability to sway the team.

Most importantly, we need to change the way we look at the concept of consensus, within our teams and our organization. All too often our teams have come to believe that consensus is a foregone conclusion if certain team leaders, executives or role models have already agreed to a course of action or plan. How many times has someone failed to voice their concerns simply because he or she assumed that the plan was a fait accompli once you presented it?

Teaching our teams that consensus happens only when all potential challenges and issues have been addressed seems like a simple shift. But it's a shift that can and will make a positive difference in your ultimate results.

Shift Into Action

We can take some basic steps to be sure we have a clear perspective about consensus, or the lack of it:

- We can let our teams know that it's positive and desirable to challenge any opinion, to ask the hard questions, to step up and be heard. By modeling through our own behavior and by guiding meetings in a way that the tough questions are asked, we open the door for people to share their real beliefs.

  In some teams, stating a contrary opinion is not easy. All too often power structures within teams make dissension a difficult position. As leaders, we can offer team members a safe method for sharing their opinions, concerns or ideas.

  One of my clients simply posted an online suggestion box with each major project or topic of discussion, offering a place to comment anonymously. He was amazed when some of the comments gave the team better ideas than the original concept.

- We can also seek consensus in an objective manner. Too often we expand on whatever topic we're questioning, driving the direction of the conversation, planting the seeds of the response we desire – in effective paving the way for agreement.

  Instead, state the facts and then be quiet and listen. You even can play devil's advocate – taking an opposing position that counters whatever proposal is on the table. Then ask other team members to come up with yet another contrary position. This is a variant on proving yourself wrong. It's a great way to counter the consensus program that we humans all face. As more diverse and opposing ideas come onto the table, people let go of a single focus.

You'll enjoy a better end result and true consensus when you push the envelope a bit to be sure you have conscious and true agreement.

By getting conscious and thoughtful, we can find true consensus around new ideas that fuel business performance.

Chapter 14

We Know Best

Mindware Program
We believe we know what's best for our buyers.

Leadership Shift
Get out of those internal meetings and listen to buyers.

What if you knew exactly what was true in your markets? What if you really knew what value was compelling, what was important to your buyers and how to give them just what they wanted?

If I had a dollar for every time I've heard a client tell me all about the amazing value of his or her offering I'd be beyond wealthy. That's one example of believing we know best[13]. Other examples are all around our businesses, from the process we use to launch products to the hiring and on-boarding process to that customer event we create every year.

All too often what we believe to be best is, in fact, less than compelling to others, especially those outside of our business. Yet we spend hours and days in team meetings making decisions about what is best for those outside that team – from our customers to other employees to partners.

Influential Leadership: Ask Your Buyers

What if you truly knew what was best based on feedback from the real keepers of the truth about your value, your best opportunities and more? You can.

Shifting beyond this human habit is simple. Stop assuming we know best and begin to ask others what they think ... and then listen. The truth is really simple.

> ***Reality comes from our markets, not from inside our walls.***

Unless you're the one buying your offering or service, what you believe really doesn't matter. The reality is that everything we need to know about our present and future is in the eyes and hearts of our customers. Creating strategies in the vacuum of our own corporate legends is how we fail.

Shift Into Action

As a leader, you can instill a culture that expands beyond your team and outside your organization.

- Let your employees know that their job is not to create the best course of action or answer but to find that best course by listening to those who matter – your customers.

- Set a precedent with your teams for collecting feedback. Teach them to go beyond your best customers when seeking market insights. Send your teams to get out and listen to your unhappy customers for a reality check.

While they're at it, seek the opinions of customers that left you or that never bought from you at all. Also, gather insights from those "bluebird" customers who are using your offerings in a new and different way. They may be the key to a profitable new market focus for your business. Collect a wide array of insights and then start looking for the truths that will drive business growth.

- Instead of judging employee value based on what they think, value them based on how well they listen and apply customer knowledge to create success. Visibly reward team members who gather and share independent market information and insights as part of their due diligence on ideas or concepts. Make it clear that what we think inside the building isn't important. What our buyers and markets want and believe is what matters.

A few simple shifts in where and how your team gathers feedback and information can make a significant and positive shift in your organization's ability to identify and create breakout value for bottom- line growth.

Chapter 15

That's My Job

Mindware Program
When things get tough, hang onto your turf.

Leadership Shift
Make team, not turf, the safest place of all.

Great leaders know that team is a critical foundation for success. We also know that turf is the enemy of team. Yet turf is part and parcel of a threatening world and survival mind.

That's why avoiding those turf instincts is a challenge for leaders in today's uncertain world. Uncertainty triggers everyone's threat responses and we move into defensive mode. Part of that defensive response is to hunker down and protect our turf, including our roles, responsibilities and the way we've always done it.

The Turf Triggers

We've all felt our unconscious turf trigger from time to time. For example:

- Have you noticed the near-immediate response to push back when someone tells you that you "have" to do something in your job?
- Or perhaps you felt that desire to react when a new team member steps into your process and changes things suddenly?
- Then there's the new boss who asks a question about how and why you do something the way you do. Can you remember a question like that sending your brain into defensive mode?

All of these and more are examples of the turf response in action.

Influential Leadership: Focus on Team

Individuals who fall into protecting their individual turf lose sight of business and personal goals. Yet traditional leadership approaches often trigger a turf response. How?

- We've all been the subjects of the wheel-and-spoke leader. They are the wheel in charge and we are all spokes with tiny portions of turf granted by the big wheel. That approach didn't work for you, now did it?
- Then there's the seagull leader who swoops in, looks for all of the problems or issues, throws out orders and disappears into the sunset. These leaders leave behind the perfect setup for turf battles over who's wrong and who's right – and the team fragments.
- Last but not least is the turf leader who consciously pit employees or teams against each other with the idea that competition fuels performance. Talk about breeding turf wars.

When it comes to teams, simple shifts can and will create greater team interaction, flexibility and unstoppable performance. In most cases, it's simply a matter of focusing on how to create a drive toward teaming up versus hunkering down.

Shift Into Action

Here are three simple examples of shifts that will produce more team and less turf.

Change your language. How we say something is more important than the words we use. A simple flip from directive to suggestive statements will shift the dynamic from threatening to feeling included. Instead of telling employees they "*have to*" do something, use a suggestion. "*I wonder what would happen if we did this? What if we could improve by trying that?*" Simple shift, big results!

Give the wheel to the team. Instead of focusing on giving each person an individual area of responsibility, present the entire wheel (aka project) as the team's responsibility.

Put team members in charge of the overall goal, empower them to decide how best to create that wheel. Stay along as their guide, but arm them with the full picture and the opportunity to create the plan.

Let them decide how to best allocate the roles and responsibilities. Make it clear that there is only team success (or failure).

Then visibly support and reward those who work together. If individuals pop out attempting to create their own turf, use a carrot to bring them back to a team focus. Make it clear that the team is the path to success and rewards.

Feed the T in your Team. Common understanding and communication can reduce the power of turf. The more people understand how others in the team contribute, the more they tend to integrate versus create turf.

Mix and match team assignments, creating connections between all your team members.

If you know two team members are jousting for turf, put them together until the turf transforms into team.

Shift assignments to give your employees the chance to understand others' roles and how everyone contributes to the over-arching goal of your business, not just their individual roles, responsibilities and goals.

Chapter 16

But That's the Way We've Always Done It

Mindware Program
Hang onto the way we've always done it.

Leadership Shift
Focus forward. The past does not predict your future.

What if you could make every decision, take every action in your business based on the reality in your market today and the trends of tomorrow? What if you could notice subtle shifts that create breakout opportunities for you and your value? What if you could see and capture emerging market opportunities before your competitors even know it happened? You can, when you ditch the way you've always done it.

Our brains are literally wired to hang onto the past. That holds true in business since we were all taught in business school to leverage trends from the past to predict the future. That might work in eras of stable and steady change. In today's dynamic and ever-changing economies and markets, it's the kiss of death.

Pilots are a great example of leaders who work in a dynamic world. That's why I used them as the model of success for my book, Defy Gravity. Pilots work in one of the most dynamic environments of all; everything changes all the time, from the wind, to the air, to the storms to whatever else may come along.

Do you think a pilot bases what he's going to do next in flight upon what happened 100 miles ago? I hope not! That glassy air may soon be superseded by bumpy stuff. I want that pilot focused forward.

Similarly, pilots don't look at yesterday's flight plan and automatically assume it's appropriate for today. They check for the reality of today, shifting the plan to match what's true *at this moment*, and then they move forward.

Influential Leadership: Forget the RearView Mirror

Our dependence on our rearview mirror can be seen in many areas across our businesses:

- <u>We rely on the way we've always done it as our go-to approach</u> for everything from creating a new plan, product, data sheet or sales tool. It's human nature to do just that, but that doesn't mean it's the best approach.

    Ask yourself, how often do you pull out last year's plan and begin updating instead of starting with a blank whiteboard and brainstorming for tomorrow? You probably do the same thing for every piece of marketing material, sales processes and product definitions.

    There's nothing wrong with that approach. It's simply basing our future on the past. I don't think that's the best approach for growth in a dynamic market, do you?

Instead, what if you started with a blank whiteboard for every new plan, materials, product design and more? What if you consciously worked from a place of innovation and new ideas, rather than relying on yesterday's news?

- <u>We target customers today based on our past successes</u>, even if those customer profiles aren't our best target for the future. How often do we assume the same customer uptake over the same period of time for a new product or service? When was the last time you looked for an entirely new market for your offerings?

Once again, there's nothing wrong with targeting our current customers with new products and great service.

Imagine how we could increase our results if we expanded beyond yesterday's customers and into the new and emerging markets of today and tomorrow? What if we focused on those bluebirds that fly into our business, seeking our next big market opportunity instead of wondering why that rep ever sold that deal?

- <u>We avoid markets because we failed in the past</u>. Let's say we took that brave step and it didn't go so well. How often do we go back and try again? Most likely we decide that we can't do well in that market and we put it into the never again pile.

What if we were ahead of our time and that market is ripe for our success right now? What if we needed a slight tuning in our packaging or distribution to create breakout success today?

We should learn from our mistakes. But that doesn't mean we abandon opportunity markets forever based on past mistakes.

- <u>We assume our value based on yesterday's feedback</u>, even if the world and market has moved on. How often have you marched into a new prospect with the value positioning from yesterday's customer, only to find that value wasn't that important to this new player?

Our buyers and markets change continuously. So must our value. If we rely on yesterday's value to create tomorrow's growth, we might be in for a big letdown.

What if we went out to our newest customers, prospects who barely know us and markets of tomorrow to define our value? What if we faced forward to define our unique benefits for future markets, instead of yesterday's?

- <u>We forecast our future based on numbers and trends from the past.</u> But what if those trends are no longer true thanks to an ever-shifting economy and marketplace.

The past cannot predict a successful future in today's dynamic markets.

That's why it's time to ditch that rear-view mirror. Yes, we can gather useful and appropriate lessons from our past. But then we need to break with the past and begin applying those lessons to our present and our future.

Shift Into Action

Twenty-first century leaders motivate and inspire their teams to focus forward. How?

We model the behavior we want from our teams:

- <u>We begin to seek out the next trend</u>, the next customer opportunity or challenge, the next emerging market. For example, instead of pulling out last year's plan and updating it, we gather the team together and begin with a brainstorming session around the best approach for today and the future. Then we use last year's information as a reference.

- <u>We question everything.</u> By questioning the knowns of the business, eliminating sacred cows and probing into the new and innovative, we inspire a future focus and out-of-the-box thinking.

- <u>We visibly reward those</u> who step into new and different thinking, those who seek that which we do not yet recognize, who bring the future into our today in ideas that fuel innovation.

The past may have been a good prediction for the future when our markets were slow to change. In today's world, that's no longer the case. Today's buyers are in control of the buying process; their needs and focus change faster than ever. New options appear nearly instantaneously as competition accelerates.

Yes, we can learn from the past, but we need to apply that learning to the reality of our customers today.

Modern success comes from our keen focus on the needs of our markets today, and in the future.

Chapter 17

Shifting Out of I

Mindware Program
We see our world through the perception of I.

Leadership Shift
Shift into the Objective Observer.

We spend most of our lives in the I perception of life. We can't help it, we're human and that's how we're programmed. I is where we live. We filter our data, make our decisions, create our perceptions and even our memories, all based on our own mindware.

The thing if, from I, we only see what we've programmed our minds to show us. That means we miss a lot of the available data.

The perspective of I also includes our expertise. We are guided by our past experiences and perceptions. That's what creates our conscious and unconscious mindware. The more experience we have, the more locked into that experience we become.

That's the problem. Our expertise creates a double bind that we can only exit when we consciously step beyond our "knowledge" and into a fresh and objective perspective.

Influential Leadership: Shifting Out of I

When we shift out of I, we access a wealth of new and diverse data. As we expand our data about our worlds, we expand our minds and our options. That's a very good thing.

So how do you shift out of I and into a broader perspective even with all your experience? Here's an exercise, called the Perceptual Positions.

Perceptual Positions

Imagine you're in a negotiation with another person (or persons). Or perhaps you're having an internal dialogue about a decision you have to make. Or maybe you're in a group discussion about an executive strategy plan. In any of these cases, there are 3 perceptual positions.

1st position: You're in the 1st person, looking at whatever you're discussing or doing from your own perspectives and beliefs. From this position, you focus on your own viewpoint.

2nd position: Then there's the person or persons who is/are involved. They have their perspective, which to you would be a 2nd person perception. To them, it's the 1st position.

3rd position: Finally, there's the 3rd position which acts as an objective observer of the situation, discussion or whatever is happening between the 1st and 2nd position.

If you want to expand your mind with new insights and possibilities, spend some time in all three positions. Clear your internal dialogue from the I position and step into the other positions.

In the 2nd position, focus on the circumstances and requirements surrounding the other involved party (ies). See, hear, feel and think as if you were standing in their shoes. *What can you learn? Write it down.*

In the 3rd position, you have the opportunity to be an Objective Observer. You now have insights from others and yourself. Take a step back and review all of the insights you've gathered. *What do you see, hear, feel and think about the situation? What fresh insights did you gather? Write them down.*

Then step back into the I position. Notice the expansion in the way you perceive the situation, the way you think about it and the new information now available to you. Can you feel the shift from I to a broader and more 350 perspective?

Shift into Action

When we get objective, we can watch our actions, our thoughts and our decision process without attachment. That's when we can *also* apply the appropriate facets of our expertise to the real situation at hand, free of assumptions based on our past.

The question is, *"How do I get objective and stay objective."* Especially if your unconscious mind is constantly automating your thought processes and responses based on your past?

Here are three ideas I suggest for clients in their quest to be an Objective Observer.

1) Get Conscious: Before you can change anything, you have to be aware of it. Start by paying attention to yourself; your responses, reactions and thoughts throughout your day. Just sit back and notice. Become aware of the things that trigger certain behaviors or thinking. Notice that process that you automatically start before you even consciously know you're doing it. Take note of that market fact that you know is true because it's always been true. These are evidence of your unconscious stepping in to automatically respond with a big fat known. Whenever you see this happening, pay attention.

2) Go Blank: When you notice an autopilot play in action, stop. Take a step back and start again from scratch. Instead of pulling that strategy plan out to update it, start with a blank piece of paper. Rather than drawing that same old product process on the board, start with a blank whiteboard and consciously look at the goal from all three perceptual positions – as your business, your competitor and that objective observer. Don't allow any knowns, past experiences or corporate legends onto that blank space. Only objective facts are allowed into your blank space. Let those facts form the basis of your objectivity.

3) Walk Away: Sometimes the best way to get objective is to get out of your comfort zone. I like to go someplace where I can gather fresh insights. Talk to a new customer, brainstorm with friends who work in very different businesses, go listen to your sales or customer service team in the bullpen and tap into *their* reality. Getting out of our own four walls and into a different environment gives us the distance we need to get and stay objective.

As the objective observer, our powers of logic, innovation, and creativity are kicked into overdrive. When we're released from the limiting programming of the way we've always done it – there are no limits to the possibilities we can envision.

Section Two Summary

As leaders we can significantly enhance our business and team performance when we leverage the power of our human minds to fuel productivity, innovation, communication and collaboration.

By understanding the mindware programs that limit our ability to see new opportunities, create breakout innovation, clearly communicate and consciously analyze our assumptions – we will improve the bottom-line results of our business.

The following table is a summary of the programs and shifts presented in Section Two. Use it as part of your leadership toolkit. Your results will speak for themselves.

PROGRAM	SHIFT INTO ACTION
We assume we're right and seek evidence to prove it.	• Search for evidence to prove your assumptions wrong. • Goal your teams to find contrary evidence. • Model a contrarian approach yourself. • Reward team members who seek balanced information.
We focus on the problems.	• Focus on the solution. • Focus on what's working within your team & organization. • Model what's working in other organizations, within and outside of your industry.

Section Two Summary

PROGRAM	SHIFT INTO ACTION
Status Quo Bias. We hang onto the way we've always done it.	• Make the status quo unsafe. • Ask open ended, "What if?" questions. • Get people involved in defining the change. • Put yourself in others' shoes, see thru their eyes. • Start with a blank whiteboard, no status quo allowed.
We get stuck in a negative mindset.	• Model the ability to focus on the positive opportunities. • Model an attitude of opportunity. • Shift your rewards to focus on positive stories and attitudes. • Reward Change visibly.
We tend to be overconfident about our results.	• Downsize projections and forecasts. • Validate with a wider and more diverse audience. • Forget the best case and focus on reality. • Build more options into your planning cycles. • Build cushion into your numbers and schedules.
We create patterns and see what we expect to see.	• Shuffle the deck. • Change the way you view your data, reporting, customer information, product information and more. • When we change the way we see and take in information, we force our mind to actually see what's there, not what we expect to see.
Our brain releases chemicals to keep us with the herd.	• Model for your teams by stepping away from the herd. • Reward team members who step away from the herd.

Section Two Summary

PROGRAM	SHIFT INTO ACTION
Mental accounting means we value some dollars more than others.	<ul><li>Don't create special categories for special investments.</li><li>Hold strategic and tactical investments equally.</li><li>Apply spending rules equitably across all projects.</li></ul>
We get stuck in the effect side of the equation.	<ul><li>Step into being the cause for everything in your world.</li><li>Teach your teams to do the same.</li></ul>
We avoid failure and blame others.	<ul><li>Redefine Failure. There is no failure, only feedback.</li><li>Seek failure as an opportunity to learn and expand for even stronger success.</li><li>Teach teams that failure is a step toward success.</li><li>Do not allow blame into your teams.</li></ul>
We assume consensus.	<ul><li>Check agreement specifically with individuals.</li><li>Test with a broader audience.</li><li>Reward team members who question and challenge.</li><li>Stay objective and teach your teams to do the same.</li></ul>
We think we know what's best in our markets.	<ul><li>Ask your buyers. They spend dollars. You don't.</li><li>Set a precedent for a balance of feedback, pro and con.</li><li>Goal employees based on their insights from market interactions, not only their own special opinions.</li><li>Let teams know the goal is to find the best answer from whatever source, not to come up with the answer internally.</li></ul>

Section Two Summary

PROGRAM	SHIFT INTO ACTION
Our brain answers threats with a turf response.	• Change your language, from telling to questioning. • Empower your teams to control the project. • Mix and match team assignments. Create flexible teams that have no turf.
We look to the past to define our future.	• Learn from the past. • Focus on the future and that reality. • Reward team members who create new ideas based on today and tomorrow. • Start with a blank whiteboard, leave last year's plan in the drawer.
We see the world through the viewpoint of I, which limits our perspectives.	• Shift into all 3 perceptual positions, gather new insights and data. • Teach your teams to do the same. • Spend as much time as you can seeing, hearing feeling and thinking as an Objective Observer. • Learn to get conscious, go blank and walk away to stay in the Objective Observer.

Section Three

What Makes People Tick?

How to Positively Influence Every Member of Your Team

Chapter 18

Insights from our Mindware

Preference programs are part of our unconscious mindware. We're all born with similar innate preference-programs structures that determine how we behave and respond to our world. We then individually tune our preference-programs as we experience and learn in our lives.

Understanding and identifying the preference programs that drive the individuals in our teams has a huge impact on our motivation, focus and ultimate results. By leveraging the power of preference programs, we will hone our leadership styles to fuel dramatically improved individual and team results.

Preference Programs Basics

Think of preference programs as the operating system of our preferred responses in life. Preference programs are content-free, meaning they don't have a specific experience or story around them. They simply exist across all of our stored memories and data and guide our responses to our reality.

Preference programs are also completely unconscious. They act on our data selection and decisions about our behavior and beliefs without our ever knowing they are in play.

When we understand preference programs, we get a look inside the processes that drive each of our individual decisions, behaviors, responses and just plain reactions to our world. Preference programs also guide our preferences for everything around our daily lives, from what we do to why we do it.

Leadership and Preference Programs

As leaders, understanding human preference programs gives us deep insights into the engrained responses, thought processes and preferences that drive our employees.

For example, some people are motivated by moving *toward* something. Others are motivated by moving *away* from something. By understanding this simple preference programs, you will be in a position to more powerfully motivate and inspire the individuals on your teams. That's just one facet of our powerful preference programs!

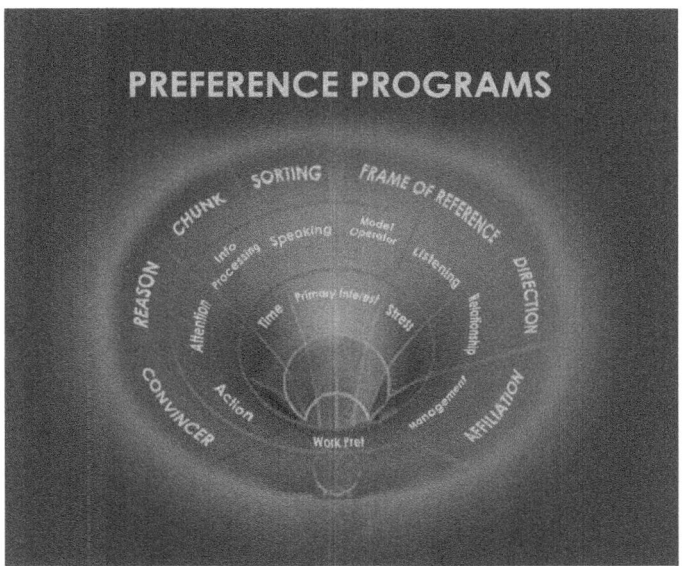

More than 20 identified preference programs determine our behaviors and preferences. We'll discuss a few select programs in terms of leadership and empowering performance in the next chapters.

If you'd like to know more about the other preference programs that directly influence our decisions and behaviors, you can reach me through my website at www.rebelbrown.com! I'm happy to share more information with anyone who wants it.

Chapter 19

What's Your Motivation Direction?

Mindware Program
Toward or Away

Leadership Shift
More effectively motivate and inspire your teams.

Since we already mentioned it, first up in our discussion is the direction filter, aka, the toward or away program. Understanding this program empowers leaders to know exactly how to best motivate individuals, their peers and those farther up the ladder.

We each define our specific mindware program along the continuum between toward or away. The infrastructure is imprinted in our minds when we're born. It's through our experiences in life that we adapt this infrastructure to our specific alignment.

Influential Leadership: Leading with the Toward and Away

As leaders, we can adapt our style to match team member's preferences. How?

Watch the behavior when individuals are presented with a stimulus, for example a positive goal (toward) or a negative motivation (away). Listen and notice how they respond and you'll learn what motivates individuals. Then you can begin to motivate each individual according to his or her specific programming. You'll see a range of behaviors.

- *Toward* preference programs. Let's say you discover that an employee has a toward program. To best lead that person you can create compelling goals, paint the picture of the *toward* opportunity. When we match the *toward* opportunity to the specific individual, we inspire and motivate. By the way, some folks are toward with a little away, which means you may also need to add a bit of away stimulus to produce the best results.

- *Away* preference programs. The best motivation for an *away* motivated player is to explain why we need to shift/change. That doesn't mean creating a threat. It does mean explaining with logic and reason why moving away from a behavior or process or belief is a positive opportunity. Finding the logical away reason that resonates with each individual adds to the power of our motivation and the ultimate results. Some people are away with a little toward. In these cases you'll need to add the hint of an opportunity to achieve the best results.

- _Toward_ and _Away._ Some people are equally balanced between toward and away. You'll need to use both a goal and an away stimulus to best influence these folks.

We each exist somewhere on the continuum of toward or away.

How powerful is it to know that we leaders can match our specific motivation styles to the needs of each individual's program?

Now that's inspired leadership!

Chapter 20

Everyone Has a Preference

Mindware Program
How we prefer to work.

Leadership Shift
Fuel ultimate productivity from everyone on your team.

By understanding our employees' preferred work styles, we can create an environment that provides them the opportunity to do their best and most productive work. In today's flexible workplace, this mind program offers more opportunities than ever before to maximize employee productivity.

Work Style Options

We all have a Work Style preference programs that defines the environment and work situation which supports our best results. Some of us seek quiet and introspection, some need constant external stimulation.

When we work in our ideal work environment, we flourish. When we are forced to work in a style that is uncomfortable or outside of our programming, we won't deliver our best results.

Influential Leadership:
Match People with their Best Situation

Some of us are loners. We work best in quiet spaces with little interactions or external distractions. Put loners in a busy office and they have a hard time concentrating or creating. Put them in a quiet solo environment and they'll produce quality work.

Some of us need lots of interaction. We need the stimulus of others, the water cooler conversations and bustling energy of a busy office space to do our best work. Put these folks in a solo environment and their creativity decreases, as does their job satisfaction.

Some of us need a blend. Some people need the solo time to create and produce. Then they need time with others to interact and gather new insights and data. The internet and social media has blessed all of us with the ability to flourish in this work style. We can create in the quiet of a home office, yet anytime we need a shot of people interaction, we can simply log on!

Matching the work environment to the needs of individual work styles enhances team performance. Think about your own style and then ask yourself if you get better results in certain environments than in others. I bet you'll find your own work style preference empowers you to better productivity.

How do you find out which style your employees prefer? Ask them!

Simply inquire about a work situation when they were the happiest and when they knew they were in their "groove" of optimum performance.

Listen, watch and learn what works best for them.

Then, give your team members the environment they need. They'll give you back the results you want.

Chapter 21

The Why Behind What We Do

Mindware Program
What motivates us to do what we do.

Leadership Shift
Match people with their best roles for success.

Understanding why people decide to do what they do offers deep leadership insights into their focus and motivation. We can use this filter to match people to their best roles in our organization and to motivate and inspire their best performance.

Our Reason filter, also known as the Possibility or Necessity preference programs, is one of the filters we use in our decisions to take action.

If you ask people why they do what they do in their lives, you'll get a variety of answers. Some folks chose their career because it was something they had to do to pay the bills. Others chose their profession because of the possibilities to change the world, make a difference, interact with new people and so on.

That's the simple difference between a person motivated by Necessity versus Possibility.

<u>People motivated by necessity do things because it's what they have to do.</u> They don't create big future visions – they take life as it comes and deal with things as they come. When they need something new, they find out what's available, accept what's there and move along.

Folks who act on necessity tend to stick with what they have as long as it's working. They'll stay in the same job, home, relationship or car until it's necessary for them to change. They like what's safe, known and comfortable. That's why high necessity folks tend to stay at the same company for years and years.

If you want to motivate this person, show them why something is necessary and important. They'll do the rest.

<u>People motivated by possibility do things because they want to do them.</u> These folks see the endless possibilities and the opportunity for development of new things as part of evolution.

Possibility folks are constantly seeking new things, new experiences and new ways of being. They tend to be restless, constantly seeking the new and different stimulus and are risk takers. That's why high- possibility folks tend to move between jobs and/or companies frequently.

If you want to motivate this person – show them the limitless options and potential of the project you have for them. They'll light up and step into their best results.

<u>Some of us filter in both ways.</u> We don't always filter in one way or another, depending on the specific situation. In our business we may filter based on necessity: in our personal life we may choose our lifestyle and mate based on the possibilities we see.

As leaders we need to determine how someone is responding to a specific project and then him or her accordingly.

Influential Leadership: The Right Role for the Right Person

How folks are motivated through possibility and necessity also offers us insights into effectively matching individuals to job requirements. For example:

- Necessity folks often form the backbone of any organization's culture. They come on board and remain for years and even decades. If you're filling a job that needs longevity, pick the necessity candidate. If you need to know exactly what needs to be done and that it is done, pick necessity. When you have essential tasks, necessity is your choice.

- Possibility folks are the visionaries, those folks who start that new division on a shoestring, who step into an unknown opportunity and thrive on the risk. If you need a cheerleader to show the rest of your organization the excitement in that new product, or to engage your buyers with the opportunities from that new product, the possibility candidate is your best choice.

When you understand why people do what they do, you gather keen insights into their best roles and the best ways to motivate them.

Simply ask why they do what they do and then listen.

Then, apply your newfound awareness of their special mindware to place them in the best role, offer them well-matched responsibilities and motivate them to their ultimate performance.

Chapter 22

What Does it Take to Convince You?

Mindware Program
How are we convinced about something?

Leadership Shift
Move your teams to agreement, easily and effectively.

Understanding a person's convincer strategy lets you know exactly what and how you can move them to agreement. This strategy is important for all of us as we communicate and collaborate in our modern world.

We've all met someone who only needs one or two pieces of evidence to be convinced about our strategy, product, service or approach. We've also met someone who took every bit of evidence we had and still needed more to be convinced.

Welcome to the convincer strategy. Our convincer strategies determine what it takes to convince us of anything – from a good idea to a good person to a good job. We all have our own unique convincer strategies. We may also have different strategies for different types of situations.

Understanding what it takes to convince someone is a great skill for all of us. Imagine knowing exactly how to convince others of the value of your idea or offer. Then imagine being prepared with the exact insights and information they need to come on board and stay on board.

Influential Leadership: Applying the Convincer Strategy

Each of our convincer strategies has two parts. Part one is focused on the way we become convinced. Part two tells us the number of times we need to be convinced.

What Convinces Us?

Our senses drive our individual convincer strategies. Once we understand which sensory data others need to be convinced, we understand what we need to show, tell or share to gain their agreement.

How do we learn how they are convinced? Ask them a few questions about how they were convinced about a recent belief, behavior or decision. For example:

Think back to a time when you had a great boss. How did you know that person was a great boss?

    *Did you **see** something that convinced you?*

    *Did you **hear** something?*

    *Did you get a **feeling**?*

    *Did you **read** some information?*

People may give responses that cover more than one sensory input. For example they may need to *see*, then *read* something. Or they may need to *hear* about your idea, then *feel good* about their decision. In the first case you need to give them visual information first, then details and facts to read. In the second case you need to tell them about your idea or project for them and then use the appropriate motivational style for them to feel good about it.

Once you understand that type of information someone needs to be convinced, you then want to know how many times it takes to convince the person using that information.

For example, let's say one of your team members needs to hear from three other people before they are convinced about the validity of an idea. What does that mean to you?

It means you need to have three other team members on board before you approach this person about the change or the idea. As soon as you approach him or her, have the other three folks ready to voice their approval and support.

Let's say you have a customer who needs to read a 3rd party opinion before they are convinced. That means you need to have that independent evaluation ready to hand to them as soon as you present your idea.

Once we understand someone's convincer, we have the information we need to guide them to come on board, fully.

How Often Do we Need to be Convinced?

The second facet of our convincer relates to time. How much time, how many repetitions and how consistently does someone need to receive the required sensory data to become and remain convinced?

We can ask questions to discover this part of their strategy as well. For example, as an extension of the above question:

How quickly did you decide that boss was a great boss?

> *I decided **immediately***
>
> *I had to work with them successfully a **number of times** then decided*

*I had to work with them over a **period of time** to be comfortable*

*I had to see their positive behaviors **consistently** after I made the decision.*

Some people only need for you to prove your idea once. Others need it repeatedly over a period of time. Still others, well, you'll need to prove it every day for them.

Shift Into Action

Understanding individual's convincer strategies helps us build the rapport and trust we need to act as successful leaders. Aside from knowing what it takes to convince someone, we can also give specific attention to each of our team's needs. They'll feel more comfortable with us and their role, which will drive productivity and performance.

For example:

- For those that require constant convincing, you'll know that you need to do or share something every day to keep them involved and motivated. The convincing can be about you and your leadership, about the goal, the project or others in the team. Maybe they need to be told they're doing a great job, perhaps they need public rewards. These folks simply need more consistent validation, so – give it to them.

- Other folks are easy to convince. Once you show them the appropriate information, they are yours for life. They are not really more trusting, they're simply running a different program than those who need constant convincing.

- Then there are the folks who range between the two extremes. Maybe they need a word of praise, a reminder of the value of the project or perhaps input from others that the goal is important. Whatever their strategy, give them what they need and they will stay onboard and motivated.

The convincer strategy gives leaders more insights into how to successfully create a powerful belief and trust. Whether you need to convince someone of the power and appropriateness of your product, goal or process, the convincer is a great path. By the way, it works in our personal lives and relationships, too.

Chapter 23

Sorting Our World

Mindware Program
What motivates us to action.

Leadership Shift
Motivate individuals to action.

When we understand how people sort their experiences, we understand another facet of what motivates them. With that understanding, we can better inspire and motivate them to personal and professional success.

We all sort events in our world to decide what motivates us.

- Some of us look at our interactions in terms of what's in it for us.
- Others sort our world based on what we can do for others.

We all fall somewhere on the continuum between sorting solely for ourselves or sorting for others. Most of us are a blend.

Influential Leadership: Leading with the Sort

To understand how people are sorting at any moment, watch how much attention they pay to others.

- *Can you tell they are interested and listening?*
- *Are they leading forward, nodding their heads and enthusiastic?*
- *Are they looking at their smart phone, staring at the ceiling and generally distracted?*
- *Are they willing to "take one for the team?" Or are they more likely to protect themselves at all costs?*

Watch behaviors and you'll soon understand everyone's sorting programs.

Sorting on Self

These are the people who sort the world and make decisions based on what's in it for them. You can best motivate these folks by framing the goal based on the benefits they will receive. Focus your motivation around areas that you know are important to them personally and professionally.

These folks probably aren't the best choice for customer-facing responsibilities. On the other hand, if you need someone to monitor and maintain standards or rules within the organization, sorting by self provides a keen benefit. They won't be swayed based on popular vs. unpopular decisions. The key is to make sure these folks stay focused on their specific task and don't move away from their goal, based on their own specific needs or opinions.

Sorting by Others

Motivating these folks is all about presenting the benefits for the overall organization or for their specific team. Couch the benefits in terms of their contribution for the good of the masses; show them the value they can give to others. Remember, these folks are inspired to transform our world!

People who sort based on helping others are obviously great candidates for customer-facing roles. They're also great for human resources or other "other- focused" responsibilities. The key is to provide the balance to make sure that these individuals don't become so enthralled with what others need and want that they lose sight of what's best for the business.

We all sort by ourselves and by others at different points in our lives. That's a good thing because there are times when each is appropriate.

By paying attention to how our teams sort their world, we can manage them appropriately, making them happier contributors and as we all reach company and individual goals.

Chapter 24

How We Frame Our Decisions

Mindware Program
Do we frame our decisions externally or internally?

Leadership Shift
Match the right people to the right job.

We all have a frame of reference that guides our business decisions; what's good/bad, appropriate/inappropriate, successful or not so much.

Our frame of reference also frames our decisions about the rest of our world. Everything in our world. We either have an internal or an external frame of reference, or a balance between these options.

- Internal frames of reference decide based only on internal beliefs or feelings. Internals don't really care what others think. Decisions, behaviors and beliefs arise from inside themselves. Few of us are totally internal, so folks on this side of the continuum tend to make a decision and then do an external check on its validity or on the consequences of a behavior.

- External frames of reference decide based on what others think or how the external environment will respond. Everything they say, do or believe is based on what others think. Externals are driven by whatever others want or need or believe. They can be susceptible to powerful personalities and charismatic beliefs. Again, pure externals are rare so most externals make a decision based on others, then do an internal check to be sure they are okay with their decision or behavior.

- <u>Balanced frames of reference</u> make decisions based on a balanced viewpoint of internal feelings and thoughts blended with external inputs and experiences.

Shift Into Action

Imagine you need someone to fill a new role that is all about keeping your organization on track with required standards or processes.

How do you decide whom to select for the job? One aspect that's important is frame of reference. You want someone who will think for himself or herself, apply the rules you require and not be swayed by the opinions or reactions of others. An internal frame of reference fits that bill.

Or, let's say you need a product manager to collect insights from the market about a new product offering and its best value. For this role you want someone who is able to throw away personal beliefs and opinions and listen to the beliefs and needs of your audience – aka your buyers. In this case an external frame of reference is the best option.

Frames of reference are very important when it comes to matching people to specific job responsibilities. Frames of reference also help us understand how someone is going to make a decision and follow through on it.

If you want to get the best performance out of an internal frame of reference person, be sure he or she is 100% behind the project, role, job or deliverable. If so, you'll get the job done. If not, you'll hear excuses for delays, process changes and generally limited results.

If you want to get the best performance out of an external frame of reference person, be sure that he or she sees, hears and feels that everyone in the team agrees with the direction, project or deliverable AND that the team sees this person as the responsible party. If the team agrees visibly, you'll get your work. If not, well, expect delays and excuses.

Chapter 25

What's Your Chunk?

Mindware Program
How much and at what level we communicate.

Leadership Shift
How to clearly communicate with everyone you meet.

Clear communication comes from managing our chunks – and I'm not talking about your body type.

Chunks refer to a) how much and b) the type of information that best fits our individual processing styles. We each have our own style of communicating and receiving information. Some of us chatter away in paragraphs, others share single words or grunts. We also each have a unique type of information we need to be motivated and ready to move forward. Specifically, some of us only want the big picture and others need all the details.

Influential Leadership: Matching Their Chunks

By matching the style of others, we can more clearly communicate. Here's how.

The Paragraph versus the Single Word

We all know someone who answers our question with a novel. Those are really big chunkers when it comes to communicating information. They want and need large quantities of data.

We also all know people who answer a question with a single word answer or a grunt, no matter how much you try to draw them out. These are the little chunkers who want and need small quantities of information.

And then there is everyone in between; those who want single sentences, two sentences, paragraphs and every other combo.

Matching the chunk size of another person is a proven way to create rapport and communicate clearly. When you match their chunk size you can know that you're communicating exactly the amount of information their mind is accustomed to processing. That's why I teach chunk sizing when I'm training sales and marketing folks, as well as leaders. This simple matching process can and will clarify and empower all communication.

Big Picture or the Details

Another and important aspect of chunking when it comes to leadership has to do with the type of information we want and need. Some of us are the big picture people, others care about the details.

We've all had a boss who didn't want to hear about the details of what was stalling our project. All he or she cared about was when it was going to be done.

Then there's the boss who micromanages everything, wanting to know as much as you do about the project, process or plan. That's another style of chunking at work.

When we recognize the type of information other people need to be comfortable and to feel fully informed, we can match the details of the data we share to their specific needs. That accelerates and streamlines communication. If we give big-picture people the details, they zone out and can get impatient. If we only give the big- picture information to detailed people, we leave them wanting more.

How people chunk also gives us insights into how they think. Global-to-detail thinkers are deductive in their reasoning. Detail-to-global thinkers are inductive in their reasoning. Deductive thinking tends to be the standard in our world today, yet by its nature it limits our perceptions and range of information. Inductive thinkers, on the other hand, tend to lend themselves to innovation and creative insights. Every organization needs a combination of both types of thinkers; deductives to analyze and manage the "facts" and inductives to break the mold and create new ideas, markets and opportunities.

Matching the level of information to someone else is pretty darned easy. Just watch and listen for a while. Simply share the same type of information that he or she naturally shares with others.

By the way, as a big chunker, I now understand why I feel like I'm pulling teeth when I'm trying to get a little chunker to give me the amount of data I need. The same thing goes for all those pesky details being shared with me when all I wanted was a status. I can only imagine how I used to overload small chunkers with my paragraphs of information.

What's Your Chunk?

Begin practicing as you identify your own chunking preference, and then those of others. Practice matching others' chunking styles when communicating. You'll see, hear and feel the difference in your communications! And you'll be able to better slot people into roles that match the way they reason and think about the world.

Section Three Summary

We all have a number of preference programs, filters and personal programs that drive each of us. Using one preference programs to determine how a person functions is like looking through only one facet of a diamond. We can and will gather valuable insights.

That said, the more facets of information we capture, from a variety of preference programs and observations of behavior, the better leaders we will become.

The simple insights into preference programs shared in this chapter can and will take your leadership to new levels. Try using this information for a month and be prepared for big results!

The following table is a summary of the preference programs, how we can determine our *employees'* specific preference programs and how we can use this information to fuel performance and results.

PREFERENCE PROGRAMS	QUESTIONS TO ASK	LEADERSHIP OPPORTUNITY
Direction Filter (Toward or Away)	*What do you want in a car, job, relationship? What's important to you about _____?* *Notice whether their answers are toward or goal or away from something they don't want.*	Learn how to motivate your team members based on their individual direction strategies.

Section Three Summary

PREFERENCE PROGRAMS	QUESTIONS TO ASK	LEADERSHIP OPPORTUNITY
Association Preference (Independent, Team Player, Management Player)	*Tell me about a work situation in which you were the happiest, a one-time event.* *Notice whether they describe a situation where they were independent, in a team or management.*	Create the best situation for each individual employee's optimum performance, productivity and results.
Reason Filter (Possibility or Necessity)	*Why are you choosing to do what you're doing?* *Notice – is their decision because of the potential or because they have to do this?*	Match people to their best roles and responsibilities.
Convincer Strategy (What does it take to convince you?)	*How do you know when someone is doing a good job? Do you see something? Do you hear something? Do you feel something? Does someone do something?* *Notice what they need to experience to be convinced.*	Understand how to bring team players into agreement with overall direction and individual focus areas.

Section Three Summary

PREFERENCE PROGRAMS	QUESTIONS TO ASK	LEADERSHIP OPPORTUNITY
Convincer Strategy (How many times do I have to convince you?)	*How often does someone have to demonstrate competence before you're convinced?* *Automatic* *Number of times* *Period of time* *Consistently* *Notice how they answer and note their frequency to be convinced.*	Understand how many times and how often you need to check back to keep employees motivated and convinced of their role and its validity and importance.
Sorting Our World (What's in it for me or What can I do for others?")	*Simply notice whether someone is motivated for themselves or for others.* *For example, Are they willing to "take one for the team?" Or are they more likely to protect themselves at all costs?*	Understand how to motivate individuals. Also, match people to their best roles and responsibilities.
Frame of Reference (External or Internal or combo)	*How do you know when you're doing a good job?* *Notice whether they seek external validation or internal or some combo of the two.*	Learn how to motivate and reassure team members. Understand how to motivate within the team. Match people to their best roles.
Chunk Size (Global/Detailed)	*If we were doing a project together, would you want to know the big picture first or the details? Would you need the other information?*	Understand how people think and process information. Improve communication. Match people to their best roles.

The Bottom Line

We are humans in business and our human mind processes our information, guides our thinking, chooses our decisions and directs our decisions.

When we shift into an intuitive leadership approach founded in a knowledge of how our human mind works, we have an opportunity to fuel new levels of productivity, innovation and collaboration within our organizations. When we choose to shift our leadership styles to take into account and to leverage, the unconscious mindware that is driving today's human behaviors and beliefs – we can and will lead our human teams to do and be more.

Leaders who put the technology of our mind to work for our business will fuel the next generation of performance and results.

Welcome to the shift – into the next generation of Influential Leadership!

About The Author

For more than 25 years Rebel has inspired, coached and empowered individuals and over 250 global organizations to next generation performance and profitable market advantage.

Today, as a board-certified instructor of a variety of neuroscience practices, Rebel blends the power of our minds with her deep business expertise to guide her executive and corporate clients to unleash their ultimate potential. She is a TEC and Vistage International speaker, executive coach and consultant and leads executive/team performance workshops globally. She was named one of the Top 100 Women in Computing.

Rebel has been featured in media including First Business TV, Forbes, Entrepreneur, Business Insider, Inc., and Business Week. She is a regular contributor for the Huffington Post, Switch and Shift and other modern media. Her bestselling business book, Defy Gravity, is any leaders' guide to breakout growth. Her Rebelations blog is read by thousands weekly.

Besides speaking and writing, she has over 20 years of consulting experience in shifting corporate perspectives to create breakout strategy, positioning for advantage and profitable growth. She works with U.S. and European venture firms to successfully fund and launch companies. She also ran a consulting practice in Paris for two years, bringing European firms to the United States for expanded opportunity.

Rebel is also the founder and director of the Unstoppable U Foundation, a non-profit program committed to guiding kids in this crazy world to know that they are born to be Unstoppable!

Resources

[1] Numerous studies exist that estimate unconscious control of our thoughts and behavior to range from 90-95%. For an interesting read on this aspect of our minds, I recommend the book, Subliminal: How your Unconscious Mind Rules Your Behavior by Leonard Mlodinow

[2] Learn more about the Many Worlds Quantum Theory. http://en.wikipedia.org/wiki/Many-worlds_interpretation

[3] Source: FLOW. The Psychology of Optimal Experience, http://www.amazon.com/Flow-The-Psychology-Optimal-Experience/dp/0061339202

[4] For a definition of Quantum Mechanics, http://en.wikipedia.org/wiki/Quantum_mechanics

[5] For more information on your mind's chemical responses to stress, http://health.nytimes.com/health/guides/symptoms/stress-and-anxiety/the-body's-response.html

[6] For more insights on over confidence and selective observation with regard to numbers, see Belsky and Gilovich in *Why Smart People Make Big Money Mistakes and How to Correct Them*.

[7] For more insights into status quo bias, http://en.wikipedia.org/wiki/Status_quo_bias or William Samuelson and Richard Zeckhauser, 'Status-quo bias in decision making,' *Journal of Risk and Uncertainty* or http://phys.org/news187878622.html

[8] *See* Pierre Wack's two-part article, ‹Scenarios: Uncharted waters ahead,› *Harvard Business Review*, and 'Scenarios: Shooting the rapids,' *Harvard Business Review*, November–December.

[9] There are a number of studies concerning how we make choices. Some are focused on pricing, some on testing, some on grocery store placement. Regardless of the focus, we tend to select whatever is in the middle. Here are links to a couple of these studies. http://www.overcomingbias.com/2009/01/why-we-like-middle-options-small-menus.html http://pss.sagepub.com/content/6/1/50.short?patientinformlinks=yes&legid=sppss;6/1/50

[10] For more insights on the herd instinct, see http://www.dana.org/news/features/detail.aspx?id=29338 or http://www.doctortipster.com/7812-new-study-shows-link-between-patients-conformity-and-certain-brain-region.html

[11] Read more on Wikipedia http://en.wikipedia.org/wiki/Mental_accounting or download this whitepaper for more information on mental accounting. http://faculty.chicagobooth.edu/Richard.Thaler/research/pdf/mental%20accounting%20and%20consumer%20choice.pdf

[12] *See* Belsky and Gilovich for more insights on consensus.

[13] *Groupthink: Psychological Studies of Policy Decisions and Fiascoes*, Boston: Houghton Mifflin, June 1982.

www.ingramcontent.com/pod-product-compliance
Lightning Source LLC
Chambersburg PA
CBHW051716170526
45167CB00002B/683